Assignments in
Leisure and Tourism

for GNVQ   Book 2

SECOND EDITION

John Ward

The Travel and Tourism Programme

Copy B6

Stanley Thornes (Publishers) Ltd

First published in 1993 by
Stanley Thornes Publishers Ltd
Ellenborough House
Wellington Street
Cheltenham GL50 1YW
England

Reprinted 1994 (twice)
Second edition published in 1996

A catalogue record for this book is available from The British Library.

ISBN 0 7487 2429 X

Typeset by Columns Design and Production Services Ltd, Reading
Printed and bound in Great Britain at The Bath Press, Avon

Contents

Introduction   v

GNVQ Leisure and Tourism: Unit Summary   x

Acknowledgements   xi

Unit 5: Business systems in the leisure and tourism industries

5.1	Restaurant management – documentation	1
5.2	Computer applications in the leisure industry	5
5.3	Administration systems for leisure centre contract catering	8
5.4	Administration systems in a travel organisation	11
5.5	Computerised reservations systems	17
5.6	Telecommunication systems in leisure and tourism	20
5.7	Office technology and information handling	23
5.8	Information and hotel management	25
5.9	Management information systems in leisure attractions	27
5.10	Data protection	29

Unit 6: Developing customer service in leisure and tourism

6.1	Welcoming overseas visitors	33
6.2	Customer care: staff appearance	35
6.3	Customers with special needs: wheelchair access	37
6.4	Customer care: price and quality	39
6.5	Sales promotion: selling Scotland to America	42
6.6	Customer service at a motorway service station	46
6.7	Constructing customer questionnaires	48
6.8	American Express (Travel-Related Services division): evaluating customer care	51
6.9	Plan a customer service programme	54
6.10	Customer care techniques	57
6.11	Dealing with customer complaints	59

Unit 7: Health, safety and security in leisure and tourism

7.1	Health and safety: Chessington World of Adventures	61
7.2	Health and safety: caves open to the public	64
7.3	Effects of European legislation on restaurant health and safety practice	66
7.4	The work of an EHO	69
7.5	Health and safety, and the provision of in-flight catering	71
7.6	Activity holidays: customer safety	74
7.7	Fireworks at Alton Towers	76
7.8	Security training for staff: Thorpe Park	79
7.9	Preventing business crime	80
7.10	Preventing theft in the hospitality industry	83

Unit 8: Event management

8.1	Planning a festival: Commonwealth Day	85
8.2	Organising a national festival	88
8.3	Government funding for sport in the community	89
8.4	Planning event catering	91
8.5	Planning activity holidays	93
8.6	Planning a conference – the need for a schedule	97
8.7	Hiring premises	100
8.8	Planning schedules	102
8.9	Assessing hazards and risks for an event	104
8.10	Evaluating the performance of festival security staff	106

Glossary 109

Introduction

General

This book of assignments has been prepared primarily with the General National Vocational Qualification (GNVQ) in mind, though many of the assignments should prove equally useful to students of other leisure and tourism courses.

One of the main purposes of GNVQs is to provide a national scheme of vocational qualifications which can stand alongside traditional academic qualifications and offer an attractive but rigorous alternative. They are intended to offer a broad-based approach, avoiding a concentration on very narrow vocational skills, which will better equip students either for entry into employment or progression into higher education. Consequently, assignments set on such courses need to be both enjoyable and demanding.

GNVQs are assessed largely on the basis of evidence collected during the course. These assignments are intended to generate a range of outcomes in a variety of forms. Some require student participation in discussion, role play and oral presentation; others demand a variety of written outcomes, including reports, letters, memoranda, diagrams and computer-generated information.

Many of the assignments are structured so that there are some tasks which can be done immediately, these being entirely based on the stimulus material which precedes them. Subsequent tasks will often require discussion and research and are likely to involve co-operative work. The tasks have been designed to generate the kind of evidence required for the cumulative assessment which is central to GNVQ courses.

Level of difficulty

GNVQs are aimed primarily at the 16–19 age group, but the long-term aim is to make them more widely available. Most students are likely to be on full-time school or college courses, in some cases combining GNVQs with GCSE and A or AS level courses.

GNVQs are being developed at three levels of difficulty, with Intermediate and Advanced levels likely to be in most demand in schools and colleges. Achieving a GNVQ at Intermediate level is intended to be the equivalent of taking four GCSE subjects; at Advanced it is intended to represent similar demands to those made on a student taking two A levels, if they complete 12 units, or three A levels if they complete 18. In other words the programmes are intended to appeal to the full ability range and not just to those considered unsuitable for academic courses. The assignments in this book reflect that aim by focusing on complex issues and providing opportunities for the development of a wide range of skills.

The structure of this book is based on the mandatory units required for GNVQ Advanced. Given the considerable overlap in the units at Intermediate and Advanced, however, many of the assignments should prove equally suitable for use at Intermediate level.

The leisure and tourism industry

Leisure and tourism is made up of a wide range of very different, but interdependent, activities and operations. These include accommodation, catering, transport, tourist attractions, sport, entertainment, the arts and other recreation and leisure activities. Its economic importance is proved by the fact that in 1991 tourist expenditure in Britain was around £25 billion. Around 7 per cent of employment in Britain is directly related to tourism.

Though leisure and tourism are growing industries in Britain, they are also changing. For example, traditional longer-stay holidays in British destinations are gradually being replaced by more short breaks, second holidays and day trips. Demand for a range of leisure activities has risen, coinciding with the growing awareness of healthier lifestyles. Forecasts suggest that this growth will continue, but will face strong competition from overseas and especially within the single European market.

The implications of this for future planning suggest that improving quality and value for money is of prime importance and that this can only be achieved by increasing standards of training and professionalism. Vocational qualifications have a part to play in creating a more skilled and knowledgeable work force. Schemes such as the Travel and Tourism Programme, supported by American Express, Forte Hotels, The British Tourist Authority/English Tourist Board, along with Thomas Cook, have shown the industry's commitment to improving knowledge, understanding and skills.

The importance of industry links

Though it is not a requirement that teachers of leisure and tourism GNVQ must have worked at some time in a related occupational area, it is essential that local industry links are established. Students are not required to complete a period of work experience either, but their understanding of the issues facing employees in leisure and tourism are likely to be limited if such links are not established. Students have to know what determines business success, what factors it has to cope with which are outside its control and they have to learn how to develop realistic and viable solutions to practical business problems. The advice and experience of outsiders increases the likelihood that what students are learning reflects practice in the industry itself.

Tutor Guide to the Units in Books 1 and 2

Book 1

Unit 1: Investigating the leisure and tourism industries

By comparison with the other seven mandatory units, Unit 1 covers potentially a vast amount of ground. Its scope makes it important to be selective in providing or suggesting resources. It would be easy to present students with an overwhelming amount of historical and statistical data which might prove discouraging.

Although there is no requirement to approach the units in a specific order, Unit 1 does contain some fundamental issues, an understanding of which is important at the outset. In particular it deals with definitions of leisure and tourism, with the structure and development of both the leisure and recreation industry and the travel and tourism industry, as well as with their social, economic, cultural and environmental impacts.

The assignments reflect the need for students to appreciate the scope and development of leisure and tourism both at national and local levels, as well as ensuring that they also focus on the products and services available through specific facilities.

Unit 2: Human resources in the leisure and tourism industries

This unit combines quite diverse areas of study – organisational structures, teamwork, recruitment and work standards. Some of the assignments reflect theoretical business approaches to issues like organisational structures and teamwork; some show practice in specific working contexts. Given the number of small businesses in leisure and tourism, theory and practice are often quite different!

This unit offers natural links with work undertaken elsewhere in the GNVQ scheme. The assignments which relate to work standards should highlight some general themes which will emerge in more specific contexts in Units 5, 6 and 7. Unit 2 introduces the idea of work standards. Unit 5 should show how they are administered. Unit 6 will demonstrate how customer service is the most important measure of quality for most leisure and tourism businesses. Unit 7 shows the health and safety standards which different sectors of the leisure and tourism industries have to meet.

Unit 3: Marketing in leisure and tourism

This unit focuses on the whole marketing process, from identifying customer needs through to planning promotional campaigns.

The assignments selected reflect the importance of marketing in leisure and tourism. The tasks concentrate mainly on the application of marketing principles in practice. Students have to assess the needs of real customer groups, determine appropriate marketing approaches, design marketing materials, and take account of budgetary target factors.

In most leisure and tourism businesses marketing is firmly controlled by a budget which may well be based on estimates of future performance. However, the process of marketing evaluation is not in practice always regarded as a very exact science. Apart from obvious leaps in sales figures, evaluation may take the form of personal impressions and reports.

Unit 4: Finance in the leisure and tourism industries

This unit stresses the importance to businesses of monitoring their financial performance.

Many students would benefit from an introductory study unit explaining some basic accounting practice and terminology before they have to interpret the data available in company balance sheets and annual reports. Smaller companies are likely to regard data about their financial performance as confidential, but may allow either the use of figures from previous years or figures which have been fictionalised.

The assignments look at the financial issues facing both large organisations, such as the National Trust, and small businesses, such as a family-run guest house.

Book 2

Unit 5: Business systems in the leisure and tourism industries

The complexity and variety of business systems used in the leisure and tourism industries inevitably means students can only become familiar with a representative sample.

The assignments look at systems whose primary functions are related to one of the three elements identified in the unit specification: administration, communications or information-processing. However, it is clear that most business systems combine these functions so that some of the assignments can be easily related to more than one element.

The assignments range in scale from looking at simple paper documentation to complex systems needed to manage a quality standards programme in a national business travel company. Some assignments are based on practice in a specific business context; others, such as the one on telecommunications, demonstrate generally how business systems can be developed.

Unit 6: Developing customer service in leisure and tourism

A high quality of customer service is often regarded as the most vital ingredient in the success of any leisure and tourism business. Many larger organisations use commercially produced customer service training material, such as Welcome Host, but others run their own training programmes, and ideas from some of these are incorporated into the assignments.

Though its importance is undeniable, many of the essential principles of customer service are not particularly complex and are equally important to other industries, most notably retail. The skills involved are often described in very general terms – communication, sales, rapport or efficiency – and these have to be broken down into stages and specific examples. Role plays are particularly useful in showing the relevance of individual skills to particular leisure and tourism contexts.

Unit 7: Health, safety and security in leisure and tourism

Perhaps the best way of bringing health and safety issues to life is to show how they are applied in a range of different workplaces. Hence the assignments cover the health and safety issues ranging from exploring Wookey Hole Caves to firework displays at Alton Towers.

The emphasis on regulation and legislation creates the potential for much very dry reading material. The assignments therefore concentrate on the need for regulation in order to control risks and, where possible, to eliminate hazards. Reference is made only to the most essential clauses of Acts of Parliament or Health and Safety Codes of Practice.

Many of the health, safety and security principles highlighted in this Unit can be applied and evaluated in Unit 8, where students are required to plan and run an event.

Unit 8: Event management

The elements which focus on selecting a viable event and planning it encourage group work and problem-solving and should offer regular opportunities to develop core skills.

The assignments cover extremes of scale, from the national to the local, in order to emphasise both broad planning issues and more specific practical details. It is important that students understand both the planning issues and the practical processes relating to event management.

The assignments provide a foundation for thinking about how to approach the specific events which students will choose to run. Because they are drawn from a range of different locations and are intended to appeal to different audiences, they should also help students to select viable and appropriate events to form the focus of their work for elements 8.2, 8.3 and 8.4.

Combination of units and elements

Each of the 8 units is divided into elements, but student activities are likely to cover more than one element at a time. It is equally possible to plan assignments which cover requirements in more than one unit. Research conducted at a single tourist attraction could provide a range of outcomes. For example, Assignments 2.1 and 3.6 are both based on Beaulieu. Studying a theme, such as the environmental impact of leisure and tourism, would enable students to establish links between Assignments 1.7, 1.10, 2.10, 3.7, 4.4, 6.5, and 7.4. A local study of leisure provision could lead to various combinations of Assignments 1.4, 3.2, 4.3, 5.2, 5.3, 6.10, and 8.3.

Core skills

Three core skills are incorporated into GNVQs: Communication, Application of Number and Information Technology. Like most skills, these are best developed in a realistic context; and they are not therefore isolated in this book but are incorporated within the context of a range of assignments. In other words the skills are used to tackle real problems and issues.

Because of the nature of their content, some units lend themselves particularly to developing individual core skills. Thus Communication is a vital element in Units 2 and 6, since Human Resources and Customer Service are highly dependent on it. Similarly Unit 5, dealing with business systems, is more dependent on Information Technology skills than some others. Assignments featuring Application of Number skills are found in several units but are particularly prominent in Unit 4 where financial issues are covered.

Each assignment is prefaced by an indication of which core skills it might be used to develop.

Active learning

These assignments are intended to encourage students to work both on their own and in small groups. Though resource material is provided, it generally also acts as a starting point for further research. The assignments encourage students to develop planning skills, judgement and initiative. Frequent choices are offered and students may wish to add further appropriate options of their own.

The range of activities

These assignments encourage the production of evidence from students in a variety of forms and from a variety of sources. GNVQs encourage the use of investigations, surveys, case studies and planning and designing activities. This book contains many such practical tasks, providing in many cases source material on which they can be wholly or partly based.

Planning and design tasks include the consideration of posters, notices, floor plans, itineraries, business plans, contingency plans and development proposals. The assignments can be used to generate among other things reports, analyses, speeches or presentations, codes of practice and guidance notes. Responses will be written and oral. Students are challenged to identify a range of principles, qualities, changes, arguments and issues relevant to leisure and tourism. The tasks frequently encourage discussion, in small groups and in role, in order to arrive at consensus or to identify a range of conclusions.

Progression

Since research degrees are awarded for a whole range of leisure and tourism studies, GNVQs provide a number of opportunities for progression. Apart from moving, for example, from Intermediate to Advanced level, successful students can move into higher education to follow diploma or degree courses. In some cases it may be possible to combine these with employment, so that the qualification forms part of the individual's overall training.

Glossary

Definitions and explanations of certain key words and phrases specific to the leisure and tourism industries can be found in the glossary on page 109.

GNVQ Intermediate Leisure and Tourism – unit summary

UNIT 1: INVESTIGATING THE LEISURE AND TOURISM INDUSTRIES (INTERMEDIATE)

Element 1.1: Investigate the leisure and recreation industry nationally and locally

Element 1.2: Investigate the travel and tourism industry nationally and locally

Element 1.3: Prepare for employment in the leisure and tourism industries

UNIT 2: MARKETING AND PROMOTING LEISURE AND TOURISM PRODUCTS (INTERMEDIATE)

Element 2.1: Investigate marketing and promotion in leisure and recreation and travel and tourism organisations

Element 2.2: Plan a leisure and recreation or travel and tourism promotional campaign

Element 2.3: Run and evaluate a leisure or tourism promotional campaign

UNIT 3: CUSTOMER SERVICE IN LEISURE AND TOURISM (INTERMEDIATE)

Element 3.1: Explain the principles of customer service in leisure and tourism

Element 3.2: Investigate the provision of information as part of customer service

Element 3.3: Investigate and demonstrate sales techniques as part of customer service

Element 3.4: Provide and evaluate customer service in leisure and tourism

UNIT 4: CONTRIBUTING TO THE RUNNING OF AN EVENT (INTERMEDIATE)

Element 4.1: Plan an event with others

Element 4.2: Undertake a role in the team event

Element 4.3: Evaluate the team event

GNVQ Advanced Leisure and Tourism – unit summary

UNIT 1: INVESTIGATING THE LEISURE AND TOURISM INDUSTRIES (ADVANCED)

Element 1.1: Investigate the structure and scale of the UK leisure and tourism industries

Element 1.2: Explore the UK leisure and recreation industry and its development

Element 1.3: Explore the UK travel and tourism industry and its development

Element 1.4: Investigate the impact of the UK leisure and tourism industries

UNIT 2: HUMAN RESOURCES IN THE LEISURE AND TOURISM INDUSTRIES (ADVANCED)

Element 2.1: Investigate and compare organisational structures in leisure and tourism

Element 2.2: Investigate how leisure and tourism teams operate

Element 2.3: Investigate, and prepare for, recruitment and selection in leisure and tourism

Element 2.4: Investigate workplace standards and performance in the leisure and tourism industries

UNIT 3: MARKETING IN LEISURE AND TOURISM (ADVANCED)

Element 3.1: Investigate marketing principles, activities and objectives in leisure and tourism

Element 3.2: Analyse and undertake marketing research in leisure and tourism organisations

Element 3.3: Investigate and evaluate marketing communications in leisure and tourism organisations

Element 3.4: Develop a marketing plan for a selected leisure and tourism product/service

UNIT 4: FINANCE IN THE LEISURE AND TOURISM INDUSTRIES (ADVANCED)

Element 4.1: Investigate the financial performance of leisure and tourism organisations

Element 4.2: Examine financial accounts in leisure and tourism organisations

Element 4.3: Investigate and carry out simple budgeting in leisure and tourism

UNIT 5: BUSINESS SYSTEMS IN THE LEISURE AND TOURISM INDUSTRIES (ADVANCED)

Element 5.1: Investigate and evaluate administration systems in leisure and tourism organisations

Element 5.2: Investigate and evaluate communications systems in leisure and tourism organisations

Element 5.3: Investigate and evaluate information-processing systems in leisure and tourism organisations

UNIT 6: DEVELOPING CUSTOMER SERVICE IN LEISURE AND TOURISM (ADVANCED)

Element 6.1: Investigate customer service in leisure and tourism

Element 6.2: Investigate sales and selling as part of customer service in leisure and tourism

Element 6.3: Analyse customer service quality for selected leisure and tourism organisations

Element 6.4: Deliver and evaluate customer service in leisure and tourism organisations

UNIT 7: HEALTH, SAFETY AND SECURITY IN LEISURE AND TOURISM (ADVANCED)

Element 7.1: Investigate health, safety and security in leisure and tourism

Element 7.2: Ensure the health and safety of a leisure and tourism event

Element 7.3: Ensure the security of a leisure and tourism event

UNIT 8 EVENT MANAGEMENT (ADVANCED)

Element 8.1: Propose options and select a feasible event

Element 8.2: Plan an event as a team

Element 8.3: Participate in the running of the team event

Element 8.4: Evaluate individual, team and event performance

Acknowledgements

The author and publishers would like to thank the following organisations for permission to reproduce photographs and other material:

Performe Publications (pages 3–4); Unipart Group of Companies (page 5); Forte (page 25); Bales Tours Ltd (pages 41–2); British Tourist Authority (page 43); Zac Macauley, photographer, Walton-on-Thames (page 62); Stuart Baynes Photography, Bath (page 64); British Midland (page 72); Alton Towers (page 76); The Commonwealth Institute (page 86); Princes Risborough Photographic Society (page 90); English Tourist Board (pages 94, 95); The Brewery (page 98); and for the cover photograph Tony Stone Images. All other photographs were supplied by the author.

Every effort has been made to contact copyright holders and we apologise if any have been overlooked.

The Travel and Tourism Programme

An interesting feature of leisure and tourism is its increasing recognition of the importance of education as a means of encouraging young people, teachers and parents to give consideration to what is rapidly becoming the world's largest industrial sector.

Students are being encouraged to view the industries both from the standpoint of discriminating consumers and as career options. With the aim of fostering this dual perspective, the Travel and Tourism Programme, supported by American Express, Forte Hotels, and the British Tourist Authority/English Tourist Board, along with Thomas Cook, has willingly enabled these materials to be written.

John Ward is Programme Development Manager with the Travel and Tourism Programme.

Unit 5 Business systems in the leisure and tourism industries

5.1 Restaurant management – documentation

Develops knowledge and understanding of the following element:
5.1   Investigate and evaluate administration systems in leisure and tourism organisations

Supports development of the following core skills:
Communication 3.4 (Task 1)
Communication 3.4 (Task 2)
Information Technology 3.1, 3.3 (Task 3)

Managing a large restaurant involves handling a variety of important daily information. Reservations and their precise requirements need to be accurately recorded. Staffing arrangements and duties have to be drawn up and communicated. Stock control has to be efficiently managed, since daily demand will vary according to the menus offered and the number of bookings taken. A record of each day's business will have to be kept and if the restaurant is aiming for a high professional standard, this may include an evaluation of staff performance and notes of any comments received from customers.

In addition to this daily information, the restaurant manager will also need some information for reference purposes. This will include alphabetical lists of suppliers and companies with whom maintenance and repair contracts have been agreed. Information about all staff employed also needs to be held in a form which is easily accessible. This is particularly important in a business where people may have to be contacted at short notice.

Efficient use of documentation can enable staff to give better, more relaxed service.

Reference information for staff is also important in a restaurant. Individual employees may need to look up details of food or beverages being served, for example the precise ingredients of a rarely asked for cocktail. The manager may need to refer to legal documents such as the Public Health Act in order to check the precise responsibilities which he or she has to carry out.

The layout of any documentation designed to carry restaurant information needs to make it both easy to use and easy to interpret. Seeing reservations listed chronologically may also help the restaurant to manage its busiest periods more successfully. It may sometimes prove possible for a restaurant to spread its business more evenly over a session which in turn enables staff to give better, more relaxed service. Such a list will certainly indicate when most business is being done and perhaps suggest how profits can be increased.

Your tasks

Study the two documents on the following pages – the Daily Management Analysis and the Daily Reservations – and answer the questions which follow.

1 The Daily Management Analysis

a) Why do you think it is necessary to write down the appointments and meetings which staff are due to attend?

b) Staff performance is measured on a scale of 1 to 4. What particular things would an assessor be looking for in deciding what score to record for 'waiting personality' and 'teamwork'?

c) Why do you think the margin notes include references to 'supervisory skill' and 'open management'?

d) What is an 'accumulative total' and why is there a need to record this for breakages and wastage?

e) Why do the margin notes suggest a connection between equipment maintenance and being short staffed?

f) Why are hygiene problems given top priority in a restaurant?

2 The Daily Reservations Page

a) Why do you think the table numbers are listed at the top and bottom of the document?

b) What do you think the Busy Session/Bar Chart space would be used for?

c) Can you suggest any other items to check before it was decided that a restaurant was ready to open?

d) What are lunch and dinner 'covers' and 'turnovers'?

e) What records are kept of the actual money paid by customers who have eaten in the restaurant?

f) What is a 'plat du jour' and why would the restaurant need to keep a record of what it was?

3 Neatley Court is a small hotel offering bed and breakfast terms only and containing two single rooms, six double rooms, and two family suites accommodating up to four people.

Decide what daily records the hotel would need to keep and plan a layout which you think would be both easy to use and easy to interpret.

Daily Management Analysis

APPOINTMENTS ♦ MEETINGS	STAFF PERFORMANCE ✓	Lunch				Dinner				1 very good 2 good 3 average 4 below average	1 Don't forget, staff performance closely reflects supervisory skill.
Staff		1	2	3	4	1	2	3	4		
	Cleaners ♦ Kitchen porters										2 Do this exercise each session. Open management is demanding but worth it.
	Bar efficiency									**3**s or **4**s	
	Bar personality									*action needed?*	
	Kitchen quality									*Staff training!*	
	Kitchen service										
	Waiting efficiency										
	Waiting personality										
	Teamwork										
	Booking spread										

Other	CUSTOMER COMMENTS ♦ REACTION	1 Record everything however minor.
		2 Does anything point to a particular problem?
		3 Do something about it today!

	BREAKAGES ♦ WASTAGE ♦ DETAILS AND REASONS		1 Put a price on it!
RUNNING LOW ♦ ORDER			2 Keep an accumulative total and enter it in the box.

	EQUIPMENT MAINTENANCE ♦ SAFETY	1 Keep your equipment regularly maintained.
		2 Any problems, particularly electrical, deal with urgently. Don't end up short staffed.

	HYGIENE PROBLEMS ♦ SPECIAL CLEANING	1 The new Public Health Act is not at all forgiving.
		2 Everybody has a responsibility here. Wherever you see a problem record it.
		3 Any problems indicated here are top priority.

GENERAL NOTES ♦ OTHER MESSAGES	TELEPHONE MESSAGES	
	For	From and number

Daily Reservations

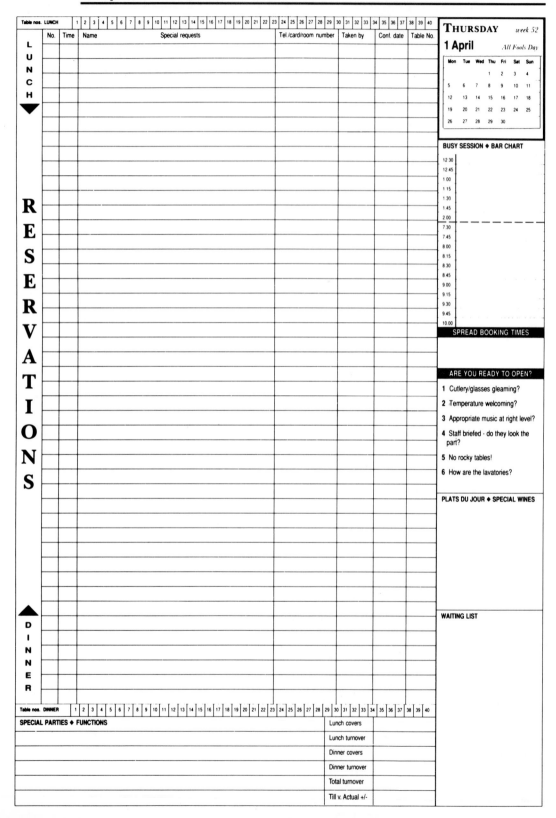

5.2 Computer applications in the leisure industry

Develops knowledge and understanding of the following element:
5.1 Investigate and evaluate administration systems in leisure and tourism organisations

Supports development of the following core skills:
Communication 3.4 (Task 1)
Communication 3.4 (Task 2)
Information Technology 3.1, 3.2, 3.3, 3.4 (Task 3)

The first point where a visitor to a leisure centre would be likely to see a computer in use is at the reception desk. Its main function here would be to record bookings and issue tickets. Accurate information about availability can be provided instantly. Where membership schemes apply, keying in the visitor's number may also reveal other information, such as whether they are entitled to a rebate or whether their membership is due for renewal.

Where a number of centres are linked, for example within a single local authority, computers can be linked in a network which enables information to be shared. This would enable bookings to be taken at one centre for use at another. However the efficiency offered by computers is only likely to be sustained if staff are adequately trained to use the systems purchased by individual centres. The support offered by the company providing the computer and accompanying software will also be critical, especially in the first few months of using the system. Software systems are usually accompanied by working manuals, but these are not always easy to understand, particularly if the user has little experience of information technology.

Computer software can devise an individual health and fitness programme.

Computer software can also be used to control access in leisure centres. Leisure centres often occupy large sites and remain open for long hours. They may have specific security problems, such as the expensive equipment kept in a health and fitness centre or the need for good crowd control at a sports ground. Magnetic swipe cards, issued to members, can be used both to give access to controlled areas while at the same time recording information about who uses particular facilities and with what regularity.

The growth of up-market health and fitness centres has prompted the development of a range of specific computer software. This performs a number of functions, mostly to do with analysing data about personal fitness, nutrition and food intake and personal exercise programmes. These programmes can analyse an

5

individual fitness session and prescribe a health and fitness programme which takes account of the age, physique and life-style of the user. Software has also been developed which calculates the cost to fitness centre users in terms of the exact amount of use they make of it.

Membership schemes probably represent the most common type of computer use in leisure centres. Their advantage, apart from speed, is that membership records can be classified in a number of different ways which will help both accounting and marketing. In accounting terms such systems enable a quick check on turnover to be made. Rapid calculations of the levels of use during each period of the day and of the impact of offering discounts during off-peak periods can be made.

In setting up such a system it is important to think of all the probable uses to which it will be put. In a leisure centre the staff may change frequently, because of the long opening hours, and so the system chosen should not be excessively complicated. Members will not want to spend hours queuing either, so the systems will need to be capable of searching for information rapidly without the user having to key in a lot of instructions first. The speed at which the chosen system works will depend on the amount of data fed into it. A membership list requiring full details of 5000 individuals will need a more powerful system than one required to keep only 100 records. It is also important that the system can generate reports in a format which is easy to interpret and useful to leisure managers.

Your tasks

A sample of four records has been extracted from the membership database of the Chalfield St Michael Golf Club.

On the following page there are four reports generated from data held about the four selected members.

1 Identify the main differences between the four reports.

2 Assuming that the whole membership database had been reported in these formats, what purpose, if any, might each of the reports have served?

3 Create your own database suitable for a school or college club membership, including fields for all the information you are likely to need.

Devise a method of generating different report formats, using selected data only, which would be appropriate for different specified purposes.

Chalfield St Michael Golf Club records

```
Record #: 1  Act: Y               Record #: 2  Act: Y
User: Johnson, Arthur             User: Millward, Marie
Membership no: 5643               Membership no: 6118
Date of renewal: 16/03/93         Date of renewal: 31/01/93

Record #: 4  Act: Y               Record #: 3  Act: Y
User: Merrington, Hannah          User: Suarez, Juan
Membership no: 25                 Membership no: 2289
Date of renewal: 00/00/00         Date of renewal: 31/12/92
```

Record I

```
Membership no User                          Date of birth
------------------------------------------------------------
            25 Merrington, Hannah           11/08/26
          2289 Suarez, Juan                 13/09/56
          5643 Johnson, Arthur              18/10/40
          6118 Millward, Marie              07/07/48
```

Record 2

```
User                        Gender Membership no
Address
Phone           Date of birth Status         Date of renewal
------------------------------------------------------------
Johnson, Arthur             M              5643
17 Hillside Crescent, Ruislip, Middlesex
(089) 577-2132 18/10/40      full              16/03/93
Millward, Marie             F              6118
'Holly Tree House', Amersham, Bucks.
(049) 465-5209 07/07/48      weekday           31/01/93
Suarez, Juan                M              2289
Stanley House, Firs Rd, Beaconsfield, Bucks.
(049) 455-6810 13/09/56      weekday           31/12/92
Merrington, Hannah          F              25
6 St Stephen's Drive, Denham, Bucks.
(089) 537-7726 11/08/26      life              00/00/00
```

Record 3

```
Date of renewal User
Address
Phone
------------------------------------------------------------
00/00/00        Merrington, Hannah
6 St Stephen's Drive, Denham, Bucks.
(089) 537-7726
31/12/92        Suarez, Juan
Stanley House, Firs Rd, Beaconsfield, Bucks.
(049) 455-6810
31/01/93        Millward, Marie
'Holly Tree House', Amersham, Bucks.
(049) 465-5209
16/03/93        Johnson, Arthur
17 Hillside Crescent, Ruislip, Middlesex
(089) 577-2132
```

Record 4

5.3 Administration systems for leisure centre contract catering

Develops knowledge and understanding of the following element:
5.1 Investigate and evaluate administration systems in leisure and tourism organisations

Supports development of the following core skills:
Application of number 3.2, 3.3; Communication 3.4 (Task 1)
Application of number 3.2, 3.3; Communication 3.4 (Task 2)
Application of number 3.2, 3.3; Communication 3.4 (Task 3)
Communication 3.4 (Task 4)
Communication 3.4 (Task 5)

Many health and fitness centres, leisure centres and educational institutions are now putting their catering services out to contract. An estimated 4 million meals are served each day by contract caterers and the top 30 contract catering companies between them generate an annual turnover of £2.5 billion.

The Sutcliffe Catering Group, based in London, has the third highest turnover of all British contract caterers, after Gardner Merchant and Compass, at £400 million a year. They manage the catering services at over 2200 sites, employing more than 20 000 catering staff in the process. Most of these contracts are in locations with over 100 employees, since numbers below this make it difficult to operate economically. The average contract will require between 8 and 12 staff, probably 40 per cent of whom will be employed in the kitchen. The others will be needed for cleaning, carrying, unpacking, administration and serving on counters or kiosks where this is required.

Though the provision of food is an essential part of the contract caterer's business, it is dependent on their ability to secure contracts with other companies and facilities in the first place. Their own business success relies on their being able to demonstrate the benefits they can bring. These can include cutting catering costs, raising quality, taking over responsibilities which facility managers may be glad to opt out of and tailoring the contract to meet individual needs. The administrative process involved in setting up new contracts is vital if a catering business is to grow. The Sutcliffe Catering Group will go through the following four stages in agreeing a new catering contract.

1 Establish whether the company or facility is self-operated or already contracted to another caterer

If it is self-operated, Sutcliffe would seek to establish a food policy with them. This policy would identify what they wanted to achieve in financial terms from the catering contract and also what they wanted to achieve in terms of providing a service to facility users.

If the facility was already contracted to someone else, Sutcliffe would seek to establish why they were wanting a change. They would want to know whether the facility manager was seeking to reduce costs or whether the personal relationship with their existing contractor had deteriorated. It would be important at this stage to establish how realistic the expectations of the facility were in terms of what they expected for their money.

2 The client submits a short outline of the catering service they are seeking

This will form the basis of Sutcliffe's plan for how the new contract will be operated. They would hope to see the location where the service is to be operated, preferably at a time when it is most heavily used. Ideally they would want to sample the food, and get an idea of the quality and portions being offered. This may not be possible, however, since the client may be seeking tenders from a number of competing catering companies and may not wish to give too much away before the rival tenders are received. Equally, they may not have informed the staff that a private contractor is to take over the catering, regarding this as a management decision taken in the best financial interests of the company overall and not requiring wide consultation with employees.

3 Sutcliffe Catering produces a catering proposal for the client

This proposal will contain a statement of objectives covering the type of food to be provided, the staff required, and the review and communication procedures. Details of menus, the number of meals to be served, staff hours, pay and qualifications, and ideas for boosting sales such as special promotions will also be included. Promoting more business within the facility is important as this will generate more revenue.

Fees and tariffs will be given in the proposal. Sutcliffe Catering earns its income from management fees charged to its clients and from retained discounts which it is able to negotiate with suppliers, largely as a result of its £170 million a year purchasing power. By retaining this discount the company is able to offer fee incentives to clients.

Sutcliffe prefer to negotiate a flexible tariff rather than a fixed tariff because the latter does not allow as much flexibility within the menu. If the daily budget is exceeded a fixed tariff means that the loss has to be recouped the following day.

4 Sutcliffe Catering talk through the proposal with the client

Sutcliffe would prefer to carry out this part of the process through a face-to-face interview with the client. This could include the presence of the team which was actually going to run the service. They would explain the proposal, clarifying any points which were unclear or which the client was unhappy about. They would normally offer to take the client to the site of one of their existing catering operations to demonstrate their capabilities and to allow the client to talk to an existing customer.

Once a contract is agreed there are still many factors to take into account if the service is to be a success. Sutcliffe will certainly monitor the contract, in case any changes are needed. They may, for example, find after some months that investment in a piece of new equipment would provide long-term benefits, either saving space or by reducing labour costs. Newer equipment might save staff time by cooking more meals, cooking faster or simply because it is quicker to clean!

External factors may also affect the contract. Changes in health and safety legislation may require additional guidance and training to be provided for catering staff. Recent European Union (EU) Directives are having a significant effect on private sector companies taking over contracts formerly run by public sector organisations. In particular the Transfer of Undertakings – Protection of Employment (known in the industry as TUPE) regulations mean that if Sutcliffe takes over a leisure facility catering contract from, for example, a local authority they will also have to take on all responsibilities for the staff employed on the original operation. Individual cases vary, but this may include responsibility for redundancy payments, pensions, and negotiation of changes in terms and conditions of employment. It can mean that the new employer has to operate the contract on the same basis as their predecessors for up to a year. The regulations can make assessing the costs of taking on a new contract difficult since a detailed analysis of the pay, conditions of service and contractual hours of work of existing employees will be required.

Your tasks

Near and Far Travel is a tour operator with offices on the outer edges of a new town. There are no pubs, shops or restaurants within a 5-mile radius.

The company subsidises a staff restaurant for its 120 employees, providing a morning service (mainly rolls and sandwiches) and a lunch service (mainly soups, hot meals, salads and desserts). Some employees bring in their own food.

The managers of Near and Far Travel are considering replacing their present catering contract in an attempt to reduce the level of subsidy they are contributing.

The following two tables summarise the existing service, its level of sales and its main costs.

Existing schedule of services

These figures are based on a figure of 120 employees on site with an estimated 70 per cent takeup of services at lunchtime and a 60 per cent takeup of morning services. The average spend per person is 65p in the morning and £1.10 at lunchtime.

Service requirement	Average daily numbers	% takeup	Average spend	Weekly sales
Morning service	72	60%	65p	£234.00
Lunch service (1200–1400 hours)	84	70%	£1.10	£462.00
Weekly sales				£696.00
Annual sales (x 52 weeks)				£36 192.00

Existing labour schedule

Job title	Hours worked	Hours per week	Rate per hour	Weekly wage
Chef manager	0800–1600	as required	salaried	£282.69
General assistant	0830–1500	30	£4	£120.00
General assistant	0830–1500	30	£4	£120.00
General assistant	0830–1500	30	£4	£120.00
WEEKLY TOTAL				£642.64
plus NI contributions				£45.48
weekly sub total				£688.12
plus training, payroll administration, insurance				£43.61
Weekly total				£731.73
Annual total (x 52 weeks)				£38 049.96
plus 4 weeks' holiday pay + 1 week's sickness cover				£3125.59
ANNUAL LABOUR COST				£41 175.55
Additional non-consumable expenditure (stationery, cleaning materials, uniforms, disposable kitchen items)				£2548.00
Management fee to existing contract caterer				£6900.00
TOTAL COSTS				£50 623.55

In order to assess how effectively the new contractor could administer the catering system, Near and Far Travel have asked for their comments on each of the following possible scenarios.

1 An increase of 50 in the workforce, maintaining similar levels of takeup.

2 A decision to employ an extra general assistant on the same terms as those already employed, in order to improve the quality of service.

3 A decision to reduce the hours of two of the three existing general assistants from 30 to 27-and-a-half.

Each of these changes might affect the catering service in other ways. For example, an increase in the workforce could make the staff restaurant crowded at certain times of day.

4 List the other impacts you think each of these changes might have.

5 Suggest some possible administrative changes which would enable the catering company to respond to each of the impacts you have listed, and note the possible financial implications of each of your suggestions.

5.4 Administration systems in a travel organisation

Develops knowledge and understanding of the following element:
5.2 Investigate and evaluate administration systems in leisure and tourism organisations

Supports development of the following core skills:
Communication 3.2 (Task 1)
Communication 3.2 (Task 2)
Communication 3.2; Information Technology 3.1, 3.2, 3.3 (Task 3)
Communication 3.2 (Task 4)

Customer service is the core of most travel businesses. In order to satisfy the requirements of customers, companies need systems which both identify what these needs are and also measure how effectively the company and its employees are meeting them. Standards of performance in service industries can be measured by formally examining the systems and procedures operated by company personnel.

International standards for service industries have been developed and companies can register if they meet the requirements of these standards. ISO9002 covers service industries. It includes a series of documents that describe the basic activities which a quality organisation should develop and implement to ensure products or services satisfy the customer requirements.

Quality standards may be used to affect quality assurance and quality control. Thomas Cook's Travel Management Quality System identified the following essential difference between quality assurance and quality control.

Quality assurance

Quality assurance or QA focuses on preventing faults occurring, though ensuring that the job is done right first time every time. This means all individuals in the process are responsible for their own quality. To do this they need:

(i) to know what to do
(ii) to know how to do it
(iii) to have the means to do it
(iv) to measure performance
(v) to take corrective action.

Quality control

Quality control or QC relies solely on independent inspection, with testing of a product or service against a specification to see whether it passes or fails. It takes place 'after the event' in that anything failing the test has to be scrapped, creating an added cost. It is not a foolproof method of ensuring that the customer receives quality service. However QC inspections remain an important part of an overall QA system.

Most quality systems in the travel business depend on the use of manuals. These key documents contain the policies and procedures laid down by the company which must be followed by all employees. These manuals are especially important to businesses with a large number of local branches or departments since they encourage a consistent approach to the day-to-day activities of all the different business locations within the organisation. American Express Travel Service uses a manual covering 40 different procedures, including:

- sea travel
- airport services
- end of day procedures
- car hire reservations
- insurance
- passports and visas
- out of hours service.

A travel management quality system is likely to include contracts with customers, document control, purchasing, security of purchasers' property, customer transactions and records, staff performance standards and objectives, checks on services being provided, problems of failure to meet customers' specified requirements, actions to improve service, storage and delivery of documents, records, quality audits and training. The table below suggests what must be carried out in each of these areas in order to enable a business travel company to provide good service to its customers.

Contracts with customers	– details of reservations thoroughly checked – bookings checked against known customer requirements – surveys used to measure customer satisfaction
Document control	– only up-to-date documentation used – information regularly updated and amended – electronic systems used to improve speed and layout of documentation
Purchasing	– external suppliers of goods and services vetted – courier services monitored for reliability

Security of purchasers' property	– procedures used to ensure safe-keeping of customer property e.g. passports
Customer transactions and records	– reference system for every customer transaction – manual or IT systems to identify transaction at any stage in its process
Staff performance standards and objectives	– employee reviews of current practice and procedures – job requirements and objectives specified for each employee
Checks on services being provided	– checks on accuracy of stocks of tickets, stationery and printed materials – checks on customer transaction details – checks on documents for dispatch to customers
Problems of failure to meet customers' specified requirements	– identifying, recording and reporting problems – establishing the level at which the problem needs to be resolved
Actions to improve service	– documenting solutions to problems and improvements in processes – establishing causes of problems so that solutions are long term
Storage and delivery of documents	– checks on storage places and packaging processes to prevent damage, deterioration or loss of customer goods and documentation – records and signatures of receipt obtained and kept for all documents delivered to or collected by the customer
Records	– records retained for an agreed period – records should be comprehensive, legible and easily retrieved
Quality audits	– impartial independent checks on processes and written procedures
Training	– current gaps in skills and knowledge identified – instruction provided in correct methods and techniques – records of training and skills attained recorded and retained

Administrative systems in American Express Travel Related Services

A provider of business travel like American Express (Amex), has to satisfy a varied group of purchasers, not all of whom have the same priorities.

Purchaser/contact	Possible priorities
Travel organiser (often a PA or secretary)	– wants a speedy, trouble-free response, as this will only be a small part of their job
Traveller	– has personal favourite tastes affecting style and company providing travel – wants comfort/convenience – may belong to frequent traveller programmes
Company travel manager	– wants to use suppliers providing best price or perceived best value
Company administrator making payments	– wants accurate invoice details presented at the right time
Company executives with budgetary control	– wants an overall travel policy which is cost-effective and flexible

In order to satisfy this range of priorities, American Express Travel Related Services identify two critical areas in their quality systems:

- the means of finding out what your customer requirements are
- the methods of ensuring that employees can deliver quality service.

Finding out the requirements of your customers can be done in a number of ways. American Express account managers are in regular contact with their business customers and also liaise closely with local branch managers. Major customers, for example those with accounts of over £100 000 a year, are invited to quarterly forums to discuss their changing needs. Account managers will also make ad hoc courtesy calls to discuss client needs. Further feedback from customers is derived from customer questionnaires and complaints processes.

Training is very important in ensuring that employees can deliver quality service, but recruitment methods are also extremely important. In the past a retail travel company might have looked for recruits with ten years' experience of working with computer reservations systems. Nowadays they are more likely to try and ensure that their technology is very user-friendly and is not difficult to learn how to use. This means that recruitment can concentrate more on personal qualities, such as sales ability or a positive attitude to problems.

Amex uses systems to gather information about three main areas of its performance. These are:

1 financial performance
2 customer service performance
3 employee satisfaction.

Financial performance

Financial records of performance are important because the company is in an industry with many other competitors and one in which profit margins are small. Sales, revenue, costs, profit and loss are all closely monitored. As well as trying to increase revenue, companies will also wish to avoid unnecessary costs. These might arise in a number of ways:

- having to rework bookings for customers who change their plans
- having to replace staff who leave and train their replacements
- having to redo reservations because of errors.

Financial data must provide an indication of the level of errors appearing in transactions and whether an unacceptable number are occurring in any single branch.

Reports are generated from data about financial performance so that appropriate action can be taken. In a large company there may be £ millions in query at any one time. The reasons for this may include: mathematical errors; disagreements in information supplied by credit card companies and information supplied by retail outlets; disputes over lack of authorisation to travel; disputes over quality of service provided; a lack of records; or taking too long to carry out transactions or bill the customer.

Customer service performance

Accurate information about customers is important because a high proportion of the company's customers, the majority of whom are business travellers, are repeat customers. Technology is used to build up profiles on individuals and corporations. However, details about individual travellers' tastes and about company travel policies change frequently, so systems need to be constantly updated.

Employee satisfaction

Performance reviews, including a self-assessment process, are an important means of sustaining employee satisfaction. Performance reviews cover a specified span of time. They summarise the individual employee's goals and accomplishments for the period, and are completed jointly by the employee and his or her manager. They include an overall assessment, rated in terms of how effectively the employee met or exceeded customer requirements. An annual self-assessment system provides the employee's own summary of how they felt they rated their performance in terms of customer service, quality of work skills, integrity, treatment of other people, teamwork, citizenship and communication. This system provides a developing career record which is used to set goals and plan future career directions.

Information systems

The flow of information from central offices to individual branches is critical. The computer reservations system is used to pass messages to individual branches and security codes mean that the information can only be accessed by the relevant staff. Supervisory queue messages will be displayed in each branch. These should have been acted on and removed from the system at the end of each day.

Relying on electronic communication can have its drawbacks. All travel companies have to rely to some extent on the systems used by other businesses. The systems used by different companies are not always compatible. Some retail travel operations are dependent on someone else's systems, such as SABRE, GALILEO or credit card systems, so other operations' systems may be responsible for problems in giving customers accurate and up-to-date information. There is also the necessity to keep backup copies. The systems used for doing this may be costly in terms of time and storage space, and may come into conflict with financial targets.

Documents

Document control is a fundamental part of any quality system. For example, American Express may be faced with a business client claiming that an airline ticket was not delivered to them. A log system will enable Amex to demonstrate which individual from this company signed for the receipt of the ticket. Detailed information sometimes has to be stored for a long time. For example, Customs and Excise may ask, for tax purposes, for information about personal expenses from seven years back. However most records at American Express are kept for a minimum of two years and then destroyed.

Simple documents are an important part of ensuring quality customer service. American Express employees keep a number of logs which ensure that essential processes are performed efficiently. The passport and visa log, shown below, provides a record of the way the company handles individual visa applications:

Name/ Passport number	Documents sent with passport	Visa/ passport applied for	Date of dep.	Processed by: (please state company)	Date received from customer	Date sent for processing	Date back to office	Date to customer	Comments

It is important for any administrative system not to generate too much paper. When this happens it tends to result in either a failure to locate and read the most important data or in an excessive amount of resources being used up in the administrative process.

People

Whatever administrative and communications systems a company uses, their effectiveness will depend on the people using them. American Express sets objectives for its employees which focus their attention on achieving year on year improvement in their work performance. Yet this process itself requires an administrative system to ensure that it works. Goals have to be set and recorded. Progress of individuals has to be reviewed and recorded against set objectives. This process also has to be linked to the company's operations as a whole, to changes in the company's business, and to managing the individual's training and career development effectively.

Non-routine functions

Some administrative systems are for exceptional rather than regular use, but familiarity with them is equally important. Thomas Cook issues written guidance to all its branches covering a range of accident and emergency situations. These cover business emergencies, such as what to do if a company with which they trade goes out of business or what to do if computer systems go down. Other guidance relates to unpredictable circumstances such as civil unrest, health scares, hijacking or kidnapping.

Your tasks

Your school or college is intending to start up a business providing conference and accommodation facilities for small groups during the Easter and summer vacations.

1 Identify the administration systems which would be required in order for the business to operate.

2 Briefly outline the need for quality standards in each of the administrative systems identified in task 1.

3 Choose one of the administrative systems identified in task 1 and write an appropriate set of quality standards which could be applied to it.

4 Describe the process by which you would monitor the performance of the business against each of the quality standards described in task 3.

5.5 Computerised reservations systems

Develops knowledge and understanding of the following element:

5.2 Investigate and evaluate communications systems in leisure and tourism organisations

Supports development of the following core skills:
Communication 3.1 (Task 1)
Communication 3.4 (Task 2)

These systems, often referred to simply as CRS, provide central banks of information about scheduled airline bookings, car rental, hotel accommodation and the booking of leisure activities such as sport or the theatre. Travel agencies use computer terminals to gain access to this information and to make reservations for their customers.

In addition to the information needed to make bookings, many CRS systems enable travel agencies to build in client profiles. This means that the special requirements of individual travellers or companies can be fed into the system when a reservation is made. One company may wish to use only Business Class seats or it may have a policy about car hire or the kind of accommodation which staff of varying seniority are allowed to book. Individual travellers may have preferences for non-smoking areas or for window seats and this information can automatically be loaded by a single action. Most CRS systems also contain an instruction programme. This enables people working on their own to learn how to use the system by following a set of instructions and choices displayed on screen.

Galileo, probably the best known CRS in the United Kingdom, can book flights up to 331 days in advance. It can call up all available flights on a particular route, giving times, seat availability, fares, aircraft type and stopping points on the way. It can quote over 50 million fares and the airlines guarantee the prices stated as long as a ticket is purchased within seven days. Specific seats can be booked by referring to an airline seat map on the screen.

CRS systems get very heavy use at some times of the year. Many people in the UK book their holidays in January and so there are often times when a number of travel agents are seeking access to the same information. A queueing system can be used to manage incoming messages from airlines and hotels so that none is lost. Once a booking is made the CRS registers it immediately. This means it is always possible to give up-to-date answers about the availability of seats, rooms or cars for hire.

Package holidays can also be booked through a variety of computerised systems. The newest systems combine compact disk, video and personal computer so that the information about holidays can be accompanied by a video brochure of the hotel or resort. The visual display on the monitor can be changed by directly touching the screen with your fingertips. This means customers can make their own choice of resort and accommodation. They can specify the price they are willing to pay, include any special requirements such as a swimming pool and select from a number of choices offered to them. Though customers may require travel agency staff to advise them during this process, others will happily research the information for themselves, thus freeing staff to deal with other customers.

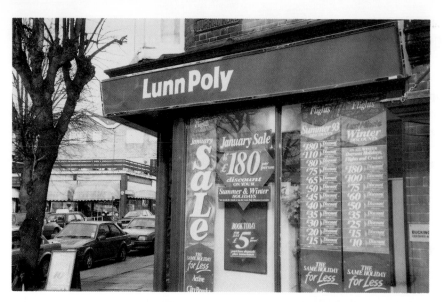

CRS allow tour operators to make special offers or promotions.

Technology has also enabled people to book holidays on the spot. Fewer staff are need to assist the booking process and holiday companies are able to deal with far more bookings than previously. For example, a large tour operator handled some two million bookings in 1987, dealing with over 100 000 on a peak day. This total was four times the number they had dealt with five years earlier.

Computerised Reservations Systems allow the rapid identification of unsold holidays. Tour operators are thus able to introduce special offers or promotions of specific destinations in an attempt to ensure that they don't end up with a lot of unsold holidays. The same process enables airlines to fill empty seats at the last minute.

The storage of information is important to travel companies. It enables them to send direct mail to previous customers. Computers can generate address labels and letters to named people at a considerably faster rate than anyone typing or writing them by hand.

In the future it may become possible to reserve holidays through a computer terminal in a shopping mall or a bank or even through an adapted television set in the home. Though this would make the booking of straightforward journeys much more convenient, many people would still go to a travel agent to book a holiday. They would want the advice and personal contact, in particular to boost their confidence in making a choice about a holiday, an expensive item from which they expect so much.

Your tasks

1 Would you prefer to receive information about holiday destinations you were contemplating visiting by means of a computerised display system or by discussing it with a travel agent? Why?

2 The table on page 19 shows a CRS on-screen display of flight availability from London Heathrow to John F Kennedy Airport in New York. Each flight is listed showing: a number, the departing airport, the arriving airport, the times of departure and arrival, seat availability, the airline, the flight number, the type of plane, the number of stopovers.

Study the table carefully and then answer the questions which follow.

    a)   What time does flight AI 101 arrive in New York?

    b)   What time does flight VS 003 depart from London?

    c) How many flights do United Airlines run on a Tuesday?

    d) Which is the only flight using a Boeing 767?

    e) Which flights use Concorde?

    f) If there were no aircraft code listed, how would you still be able to identify the Concorde flights?

    g) What code should be used to call up the details of flights into all New York airports, including those other than JFK?

    h) What reason can you suggest for the extra numeral in the flight code for the Boston–JFK flight (listed as 15); why is it listed at all?

Flight availability from London Heathrow to John F Kennedy Airport, New York

28 SEP Tue 1200 LHR – JFK New York, NY, US. Use city codes LON/NYO for full airport availability

	Departure airport	Arrival airport	Time of departure	Time of arrival	Seat availability	Airline/flight number	Type of plane	Stopovers
1	LHR	JFK	0900	1200	FA DA YA BA MA	BA 101	74L	0
2	LHR	JFK	1030	0920	R9	BA 001	SSC	0
3	LHR	JFK	1055	1415	FA CA YA BA MA	UA 901	EQV	0
4	LHR	JFK	1100	1400	F9 J9 B9 K9 A9 Q9	BA 175	740	0
5	LHR	JFK	1200	1445	FA QA YA LA	AI 101	747	0
6	LHR	JFK	1200	1510	FA QA YA BA MA	AA 105	74L	0
7	LHR	JFK	1330	1650	FA CA YA BA MA	UA 903	EQV	0
8	LHR	JFK	1415	1720	F9 J9 S9 B9 A9 Q9	BA 177	740	0
9	LHR	JFK	1545	1815	FA YA	KU 101	747	0
10	LHR	JFK	1630	1910	JA YA BA KA LA	VS 003	747	0
11	LHR	JFK	1800	2130	FA CA YA BA MA	AA 107	767	0
12	LHR	JFK	1830	2130	F9 J9 S9 B9 K9 A9	BA 179	740	0
13	LHR	JFK	1900	1750	R9	BA 003	SSC	0
14	LHR	BOS	1500	1735	F9 J9 S9 B9 K9 A9	BA 215	740	0
15	BOS	JFK	1915	2030	YA BA MA QA VA	PA 4791	DH7	0

Key to seat availability: F = first class
                              C = club class
                              Y, B, M, etc. = other classes of seat
                              9 = more than 9 seats available.

5.6 Telecommunication systems in leisure and tourism

Develops knowledge and understanding of the following element:

5.2 Investigate and evaluate communications systems in leisure and tourism organisations

Supports development of the following core skills:
Communication 3.4 (Task 1)
Communication 3.2; Information Technology 3.4 (Task 2)
Communication 3.4; Information Technology 3.4 (Task 3)

The travel and tourism industry is very dependent on the quick and accurate transfer of information. In the distant past communication between tour organisers, agents and customers would have largely been conducted by mail or by dispatch riders. Such methods of communication were slow and involved a risk of the information being lost or damaged in transit. Nowadays the development of telecommunications has revolutionised the way in which travel and tourism businesses are able to store, retrieve, receive, amend and transmit information. Messages can be conveyed around the world in seconds and information can be called up at the touch of a button.

The main systems of telecommunication include the following.

Telephones

The telephone is an essential tool in many travel and tourism businesses. Most telephones plug into a socket which links them to the public telephone network. A variety of facilities are now available on modern handsets. Features will allow the last number called to be redialled automatically, frequently used numbers to be keyed into a memory and the user to carry on a call with both hands free to continue working.

Larger businesses will probably have a telephone network. A switchboard has a number of lines linking it to the public telephone network and to a number of internal extension lines. This is a more economic way of providing access to the public system than equipping everyone with an individual telephone line.

A smaller company may not always have someone available to receive incoming calls and so the development of answering machines has helped them to avoid losing business by missing calls. The answering machine plays a recorded message to a caller, asking them to leave their own message. Some machines have a remote interrogation facility so that they can be called up from another telephone and have any messages on them played back, stored or deleted.

Modern telephone exchanges are able to provide telephone users with a range of special services which are of particular value in a business environment. For example a call waiting system can pass a message to someone using the telephone that there is another caller trying to get through. Other services can redirect calls to a different number and stop either incoming or outgoing calls.

A major development is the increased use of cordless and cellphones. These allow people to keep in contact while they are moving about. Cordless phones work from a base unit which plugs into a telephone socket and an electric mains socket. Cell phones are powered either by built-in battery units or else run off car batteries. Smaller portable telephones can be carried in pockets or briefcases but they need to be recharged regularly. Cellphones depend on a network of radio stations which link them into the public telephone network.

People in the travel industry often have to be very mobile, and a system called voice messaging enables callers to record a message and have it delivered to a mailbox. The user of the system can dial the mailbox, use a personal identification number and listen to any messages which have been recorded. The system is especially valuable for people who spend a lot of time working outside office hours or who travel in countries where there are significant time differences.

Fax

Facsimile machines, generally known as fax, are used to send messages where the receiver needs a paper copy. The machine scans the document to be sent and transmits details over a telephone line to a receiving fax machine which prints out an exact copy. One of the advantages of this system is that pictures and graphics can be transmitted as well as text.

Telex

A common means of sending accurate information rapidly is through telex machines. Messages are prepared using a keyboard and a visual display unit (VDU). A printer produces copies of the message at both ends of the system. Telex machines acknowledge receipt of messages by the exchange of a code. A business might prefer to use telex rather than fax for very important documents, since telex documents are generally accepted as legally binding.

E-mail

Electronic mail sends text from a personal computer over the telephone network. It is received in an electronic mailbox, access to which can only be gained by the use of personal passwords. The receiver of the information can either store the message in a personal computer, send an instant reply or use a printer to make a hard copy.

Viewdata

Viewdata plays a prominent role in some areas of the travel and tourism industry, especially in retail travel. A viewdata service allows users to employ the telephone network in order to gain access to information stored in business databases. Information can be called up on a television monitor, generally using personal codes to access the different systems. Travel agents, for example, may pay to use various business databases giving information about different holiday products, airline tickets, and accommodation and car hire products.

Some viewdata systems, such as British Telecom's Prestel, are interactive. This means that the users can send messages to the information providers and so use the system to make instant reservations. From the traveller's point of view the system enables them to see immediately what is available. It also often means that they can book at short notice and also compare the prices of competing tour operators or transport providers.

Videoconferencing

Travel and tourism businesses often operate in more than one country. The amount of travel involved in negotiating new business and sustaining existing operations can be both costly and time-consuming. Videoconferencing enables groups of people to hold face-to-face meetings without having to move away from their normal workplace. The system uses television monitors with built-in cameras to enable participants to see and hear both the spoken words of other groups, and also to view documents or data they may want to show. Pictures are transmitted over the public telephone network using a technology called data compression.

Your tasks

Partners Phil Fuller and Dinah Eaton run a catering business from home. They advertise their services in the local newspaper. They specialise in providing catering for outdoor events and are therefore required to spend considerable amounts of time away from their home base.

They have had an extension built to house larger kitchen facilities and a spare bedroom has been converted into an office.

Some of their suppliers are local but they have to go to the nearest city, some 60 miles away, for some more specialist food items.

Over the last year Phil and Dinah have set up a consultancy service. This arose from contacts they made during a holiday in Eastern Europe, and has developed into a number of contracts to provide small businesses with advice and guidance about how to set up and manage their affairs. Contacts established in carrying out this work have led to offers of similar consultancy work in Indonesia and Malaysia.

1 Propose a telecommunications system which you think would meet all the business needs of Phil and Dinah.

2 Explain the main advantage to the business of each piece of communications equipment you included in the system you outlined in task 1.

3 It is likely that many of the communication needs you identified in task 1 were intended for contacting external sources. What kind of internal communication would be necessary between Phil and Dinah, and what system would you suggest for ensuring that internal communication was accurate and efficient?

5.7 Office technology and information handling

Develops knowledge and understanding of the following element:
5.3 Investigate and evaluate information-processing systems in leisure and tourism
organisations

Supports development of the following core skills:
Application of number 3.1; Information Technology 3.1 (Task 1)
Information Technology 3.2, 3.3, 3.4 (Task 2)

Not many years ago you could walk into an office and find it full of files, paper, letters and
index cards. Like other industries, tourism has benefited from the increasing use of electronic devices which enable information to be stored and communicated much more
rapidly and efficiently.

Filing methods using paper or card systems take up increasing amounts of space as the
quantity of paper grows. Computer databases will store vast amounts of information while
taking up little space. Finding and altering files can be done in one operation. Information
which previously might have taken hours of hunting through paper files to find can now be
retrieved in seconds. Each record in a database file can be divided into fields, each of
which gives a different kind of information such as name, address, sales record and so on.
The information in the files can be ordered in different ways, for example either alpha-
betically, chronologically or on the basis of any field within the individual records. Totals
and other calculations can be performed automatically. Records and information can be
changed without having to rewrite the whole file.

Sending messages is very important in any kind of office operation. Using postal or
despatch services can mean a wait of several days for information to arrive. There are a
number of systems now available which enable messages to be sent electronically. Telex
messages are sent by dialling the number of a company and, once connected, by typing a
message. Copies of the message are produced by the printers at both ends of the communication. A code system is used to prove that the call went to the intended receiver. Teletext
is an electronic mail service which works more quickly than telex. It can be operated
through an electric typewriter or a computer. The text is prepared on a teletext terminal
and can then be sent either to a single receiver or to several destinations by pressing the
right buttons. Facsimile machines (often called fax machines) are used as a means of sending exact copies of documents via the telephone system. This is particularly useful where
the document contains diagrams or illustrations, but its main advantage is that the
receiver's copy is arriving at the same time as the sender is transmitting it – a much faster
system than sending documents by post.

In the travel industry much communication is international. Satellite links have dramat-
ically increased the speed at which messages can be transmitted across the world. Information is aimed from dish aerials at a satellite. The message is carried by a beam which
bounces back off the satellite so that it can be picked up by a receiving aerial. In this way
information can pass half way around the world in seconds.

Storing information is equally vital to the travel industry. Prestel is a system using ordinary telephone lines to connect computer-stored information with television sets or

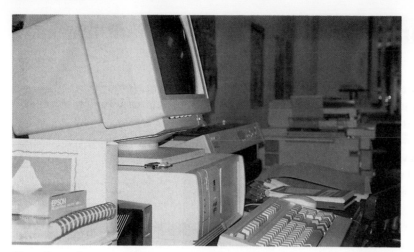

Most offices will have a range of sophisticated electronic equipment.

micro-computers. By dialling a page number, different types of information can be displayed. This might include information about travel timetables, entertainment listings, tax guides and company law. The system also enables messages to be exchanged, so it can be used to perform tasks like booking hotel rooms.

Larger companies find meetings essential but time-consuming, especially where the majority of those attending have to travel to the venue. However, letters and phone calls are often too impersonal a means of communication when decisions have to be reached which require negotiation and the establishment of trust between all participants. A system called Confravision now enables groups of people from different parts of the country to use a video display to see and talk to each other. This saves both time and expense.

Other applications of technology have enabled companies to cut the costs of sending and receiving information. Research suggests that only about one in four business telephone calls reaches the intended receiver first time. Systems can now be fitted to telephones which mean that if the person being called is engaged, their phone will accept an incoming call the moment they put the receiver down. The person using the telephone can be warned that the call is important by a bleep inserted into their conversation.

Your tasks

1 A school sports hall has up until now been used exclusively by school students. The governors approve a plan to open its small weights and fitness room to the public on three nights of the week. Funds are allocated for the purchase of some new equipment. The Head of PE at the school is given a 6-month trial period to establish and manage the scheme.
List the types of information s/he would need to gather and store.

2 Devise a system for storing all the necessary information so that it would be secure but easily and quickly accessible when required.

5.8 Information and hotel management

Develops knowledge and understanding of the following element:

5.3 Investigate and evaluate information-processing systems in leisure and tourism organisations

Supports development of the following core skills:

Application of number 3.1; Communication 3.1 (Task 1)
Information Technology 3.1, 3.3 (Task 2)
Information Technology 3.3, 3.4 (Task 3)

Information technology is playing an increasingly important role in the management of modern hotels. Larger hotels are likely to use computer-based management systems which may cover just the operations run from the front desk but which may integrate all the activities within the hotel which require information handling.

Most hotels will use computer software for their reservations and check-in requirements. This will also enable them to keep records of each guest's history and to generate statistical data to assist in managerial decisions about the hotel's future policies and practices.

Most of a large hotel's financial information will be generated by means of a computer. This has advantages for guests in that it can speed up the process of producing invoices and check-out information. Additional items such as drinks can be automatically transferred to the relevant bills and separately itemised.

Complete management systems will also make a number of other functions available. Communication between reception and housekeeping departments over morning calls, laundry, maintenance and special requests can be managed efficiently. The ordering of stock for restaurant and bar areas can be automated so that early advice of replacement requirements can be given. The risks of some of these stocks being stolen are also reduced. The system should also manage all the hotel's accounts, including sales, purchases and payroll records. It will enable management reports to be produced quickly in an appropriate format.

An example of the way in which technology has speeded

Most hotels use computer-based management systems.

25

up the transfer of information in hotels is the system of billing telephone calls. Years ago a switchboard operator would have kept a record of all outgoing calls and written their cost by hand onto the relevant guest's bill. Calls are now likely to be recorded automatically and included as an item on a computer-generated bill.

Reservations in large hotels would once have been recorded on a display board, using some system of markers to represent occupied and unoccupied rooms. This was very time-consuming, especially since much of the information had to be entered by hand into record books.

Restaurant and housekeeping managers in large hotels need up-to-date information if they are to work efficiently. The Restaurant Manager needs to know how much stock to order and how much food to prepare. The Housekeeping Manager needs to know that a sufficient number of staff is available to clean and service all the rooms required. The number of guests and the number of rooms have to be counted each day. Many large hotels have a system whereby a housekeeper who has finished servicing an individual room simply keys a code into the telephone. This connects it automatically to a central computer system which then displays the fact that the room has been cleaned and serviced and is ready for use.

More modern hotel rooms offer an increasing amount of electronic gadgetry assisting the movement of information. These may include personal pagers, in-room answering machines and remote control television screens offering everything from messages to weather reports.

Your tasks

1 Discuss the reasons why a hotel might be interested in keeping a record of guest histories.
   Identify the information which it would be useful to include in such guest histories.

2 Use a computer to plan the layout, with suitable fields, for a single record to act as the model for a guest history database.

3 Outline the specific features of an automated stock control system which you think would significantly reduce the theft of stock from a hotel. Include an indication of the frequency and type of data you would expect the system to generate.

5.9 Management information systems in leisure attractions

Develops knowledge and understanding of the following element:

5.3   Investigate and evaluate information-processing systems in leisure and tourism organisations

Supports development of the following core skills:

Information Technology 3.1, 3.2 (Task 1)

Information Technology 3.2, 3.3 (Task 2)

Management information systems are simply methods of gathering data about a company's operations in a form which helps in making decisions, record-keeping, and improving efficiency. Even relatively small retail operations, for example, may use electronic point of sale equipment which generates information not just about volume of sales, but also about how different departments and different sales staff are performing.

Organisations handling large sums of money and employing many staff have particular need of good information systems. The payroll of such a company is an area where the data is complicated and where a manual system is time-consuming. In the past employees would have used time cards which were placed into a clocking machine when they began and ended work. The information from these cards would then have to be transcribed by hand onto record sheets to be delivered by hand to an accounts department.

Computerised time and attendance systems replace cards with swipe cards from whose magnetic tape information can be automatically recorded. General principles about salaries and wages entered into the system mean that the accuracy of financial calculations can be checked far more quickly. These systems also provide other kinds of information, especially useful to organisations based on more than one site. They can keep track of employees' movements. This may in turn indicate that some work, the maintenance of a particular piece of equipment for example, actually takes longer than they had expected.

Record keeping is an essential part of the work of a personnel department. Where several hundred employees are involved, the quantity of information needed is considerable. Apart from the legal requirements, most companies store data about their individual employees' working records. These may include appraisal documents, records of projects worked on, training records and any disciplinary matters in which they were involved. Even in a single area, that of holiday and sickness records, the company may wish to distinguish between a range of reasons for absence. Madame Tussaud's, for example, keeps records which enable each of the following reasons for absence to be separately identified: accident at work, accident elsewhere, discipline, death in the family, holiday, jury duty, leave of absence, absent on business, personal sickness, sickness in the family.

Leisure parks like Alton Towers use a computerised information system for their merchandising. Once an order for goods is placed it is manually typed into the system. When goods arrive at or are transferred from the warehouse to a retail unit on the site the information is similarly recorded. All goods are bar-coded so that electronic tills can record information about their price and sale. Overnight this information is downloaded to a central multi-user system. Access to this information is available at the warehouse and at the retail offices. Access to the information is limited by the use of passwords. This means that, dependent on the employee's function and seniority, they have access only to the information which they need in order to carry out their responsibilities.

The extent to which companies invest in computerised information systems is a matter of the relative costs and benefits. In addition to the cost of the hardware and software staff have to be employed to type in the necessary information for the system to function. Training and maintenance, often provided through contracts with suppliers of equipment, have to be paid for. The benefits are generally related to increased efficiency and time saving. In the case of merchandising they can also save money. A stock control system can reduce the amount of stock which needs to be held in store because accurate orders can be processed much closer to the time they are needed. This saves storage space and, more importantly, reduces outlay by delaying payment for bulk supplies.

Your tasks

Monty's Deck Chair Service, operating on the promenade at Sandcastle-on-Sea, employs four students each year from June to September. They all start work at 10 a.m., as long as the weather is good enough to encourage people to sit in deck chairs, and continue until 5 p.m. They receive £3 an hour but are not paid whenever the service is suspended because of the weather.

Barry, who has worked for Monty in previous years, is occasionally paid a flat £10 to deputise for Monty on his days off. On fine evenings, especially in July and August when a brass band plays in the Promenade Gardens, Monty sometimes keeps the chairs out for an extra two hours, paying £4 an hour for two of the students to work late.

Figure 1 below is an example of the manual records which Monty keeps for each individual. Figure 2 opposite shows how he summarises this information for himself and his four employees.

1 In what ways might Monty use his newly acquired home computer to improve his record-keeping?

2 The success of the Deck Chair Service leads Monty to buy up the nearby seafood stall, Ever so Shellfish Ltd. Local by-laws require the stall to close on Sundays and at 4 p.m. every other evening, and not to open before 10.30 a.m. in the morning. The former

Name: **Len**	Week ending: *July 7th 1992*							Overtime	
	10–11	11–12	12–1	1–2	2–3	3–4	4–5	1	2
Monday	✓	✓	✓						
Tuesday	✓	✓	✓	✓	✓	✓	✓		
Wednesday		✓	✓	✓	✓	✓	✓	✓	✓
Thursday	✓	✓	✓	✓	✓				
Friday		✓	✓	✓					
Saturday	✓	✓	✓	✓	✓	✓	✓	✓	✓
Sunday				✓	✓	✓			

HOURS TOTAL	34
PAY DUE	£102
OVERTIME (4 hours @ £4)	£16
TOTAL	£118

Figure 1
Monty's records for individual employees.

Name	Monty		Baz			Jim		Doug		Lew	
Hrs/Overtime/Bonus	Hrs	OT	Hrs	OT	Bns	Hrs	OT	Hrs	OT	Hrs	OT
Week ending:											
Sunday July 7th	28	2	28	2	1	21	–	31	–	34	4
Sunday July 14th	35	2	28	2	1	24	2	32	–	28	2
Sunday July 21st	21	–	17	–	1	21	–	14	–	21	–
Sunday July 28th	28	2	38	4	2	28	–	32	2	35	2
Total Hours	112 + 6		111 + 8 + 5			94 + 2		109 + 2		118 + 8	
Total Pay	£360		£415			£290		£335		£386	

Figure 2
Monty's summary of employees' hours worked.

owners, Sid and Betty, agree to job share (doing exactly half the hours required each) for a rate of £3.50 an hour.

How can Monty reorganise his records system to accommodate both his businesses?

5.10 Data protection

Develops knowledge and understanding of the following element:

5.3 Investigate and evaluate information-processing systems in leisure and tourism organisations

Supports development of the following core skills:
Communication 3.1 (Task 1)
Communication 3.1 (Task 2)
Communication 3.1; Information Technology 3.1, 3.4 (Task 3)

Data about many aspects of our personal lives is held in computerised records. Anyone driving a licensed vehicle, or paying National Insurance contributions or holding credit cards will be aware that details like their name, address, income and health records may be held by organisations outside their personal control. Most people would not wish this information to be passed on, although the growing amount of unsolicited mail which most of us receive suggests that names and addresses are not regarded as confidential.

There are clearly strong reasons for keeping financial information secure, not least because of the need to protect individuals against fraud and theft. Yet even this issue can lead to conflict. Banks, for example, are legally obliged to inform the Inland Revenue of any interest paid to account holders, regardless of whether the individuals have declared such earnings on the income tax return form. Customers wishing to use credit cards to finance expensive items such as holidays find that the banks will indicate to the selling company any individual credit limit set.

While the release of certain financial information can be defended on legal or practical grounds, issues relating to personal records are more contentious. School, employment and medical records can all be held in computerised systems. Most people would agree that the individual has the right to privacy in areas such as their personal medical history. Yet individual employers might say that it would be important for them to know about certain medical conditions. School and employment records may consist of some objective data such as examination results or dates of employment and promotion. The recording of subjective information, such as another person's opinion of an individual's potential, is often extremely misleading. It generally fails to record the reasons for the judgement, cannot take into account the prejudices of the person offering the judgement and is likely to become outdated.

Personal records which are not frequently updated are also likely to provide false impressions. The security of the system being used to store the records is equally important. Backup copies of files have to be kept so that data which has been corrupted as a result of faults in the system can be quickly restored. Access to personal data should restrict the possibilities of any deliberate interference, alteration or unauthorised copying of information. There are two main ways of doing this. The first is to make physical access to the system difficult, either by using security guards or sophisticated locking systems which require personal identification to open them. The second method is to employ a system of passwords which allows different personnel access only to the data which they need to fulfil their particular functions.

In most European countries there is agreement on the broad principles to which all companies maintaining personal computerised records should adhere. They are required to:

- declare and/or register the use for which data is stored
- provide the data subject with a right of access to data concerning themselves
- maintain a prescribed minimum level of electronic and physical security in their computer system
- refuse to transmit personal data to any organisation that does not have similar controls over the use of data.

The Data Protection Act of 1984 outlined the conditions which would apply to UK organisations storing personal data. One of the first conditions to come into effect was one granting individuals the right to compensation if they had suffered damage or distress as a result of a failure to protect information held about them. From 1986 data users were required by law to register their activities with the Data Protection Registrar. In doing so they were required to explain the purpose of the data they were holding, the source from which it was obtained and any other organisations to whom they were planning to disclose this information.

Stages of the Act which came into force in 1987 gave courts the power to instruct data users to correct or erase records, where it had been demonstrated that these were inaccurate or untrue. Data users who failed to comply with a court's instructions could be removed from the Data Protection Register altogether, although this provision was regarded as a last resort. Individuals were granted the right to receive written copies of information held about them by any registered data user.

Underlying the Data Protection Act were eight statements of good practice:

1 The information to be contained in personal data shall be obtained, and personal data shall be processed, fairly and lawfully.
2 Personal data shall be held only for one or more specified and lawful purposes.
3 Personal data held for any purpose or purposes shall not be used or disclosed in any manner incompatible with that purpose or those purposes.

4 Personal data held for any purpose or purposes shall be adequate, relevant and and not excessive in relation to that purpose or those purposes.

5 Personal data shall be accurate and, where necessary, kept up to date.

6 Personal data held for any purpose or purposes shall not be kept longer than necessary for that purpose or those purposes.

7 A data subject shall be entitled:

   a) at reasonable intervals and without undue delay or expense:

      i) to be informed by any data user whether they hold personal data about that individual

      ii) to access to any such data

   b) where appropriate, to have such data corrected or erased.

8 Appropriate security measures shall be taken against unauthorised access to, or alteration, disclosure or destruction of personal data and against accidental loss or destruction of personal data.

Your tasks

1 Discuss the relative importance of the eight principles of the Data Protection Act. Then consider the implications for a large company of putting them into practice. What problems might they encounter and what solutions can you suggest?

2 The Data Protection Act does not cover files kept on paper in filing cabinets. Can you suggest any reasons for this? What difficulties might arise from an attempt to extend the Act to cover data stored in paper files?

3 A popular leisure park, primarily attracting families with young children, has 30 vacancies for staff to work there for the summer season only.

Advertisements are placed in the local press and applicants are asked to send a letter and CV.

Discuss the arguments for and against taking the following data into consideration when selecting successful applicants:
- school record
- previous employment record
- medical record
- credit status
- criminal record.

Unit 6 Developing customer service in leisure and tourism

6.1 Welcoming overseas visitors

Develops knowledge and understanding of the following element:
6.1 Investigate customer service in leisure and tourism

Supports development of the following core skills:
Application of number 3.3; Communication 3.4 (Task 1)
Communication 3.2 (Task 2)
Application of number 3.2, 3.3; Communication 3.2 (Task 3)

Any country wishing to attract overseas visitors needs to be aware of the first impressions their visitors receive. If this is a long wait at Passport Control followed by an unfriendly grilling by Customs and Excise staff, the chances of a return visit have already been reduced. If customers are to feel that their needs are being successfully met, they expect to be treated with efficiency and courtesy.

Efficiency is often a matter of having sufficient staff to ensure that queues move rapidly through passport and customs controls. The advantages which the opening of the Channel Tunnel will bring will be partly lost if there are long delays for passengers crossing from one country to another. Perhaps carrying out immigration clearance procedures on board, now available with some coach passengers, will become more common.

One method of trying to ensure good customer care is to set performance standards. The Government is to introduce these at Gatwick and Heathrow,

Travellers need to be treated with efficiency and courtesy.

33

setting a target of three minutes as the maximum wait for any EC national entering Britain before being seen by an immigration officer. Another possible method of speeding up the process is to clear visitors at their point of embarkation. This would have to be negotiated very thoroughly with the company providing the transport, but the 1988 Immigration Act does provide for **private sector** organisations to pay for extra immigration facilities in order to get a superior service for their customers.

Customs and Excise officers have the difficult task of preventing smuggling while causing the least amount of inconvenience to innocent passengers. Most arrival points in the United Kingdom present the visitor with a choice of Red or Green Channels, depending on whether they have goods in their possession on which import taxes are due. Leaflets and posters on transport and at points of entry are intended to make people rapidly aware of their tax-free allowances. Recent attempts to speed up the process include 'Red Points' where passengers can make an early declaration of the goods they are carrying, sometimes before they collect their luggage. All passengers then go through an open spot check.

Courtesy is equally important in welcoming foreign visitors. When there are delays or people need to be questioned, visitors should always be given a clear explanation. When luggage has to be searched, customs officers should offer to help repack cases. Customs officers now wear name badges (it was felt that this would make them seem more human), and their training insists that they are courteous at all times.

Midshire Airport

Midshire Airport is a small but developing airport which receives 72 incoming flights per day between the hours of 8 am and 9 pm. The average number of daily incoming passengers remains fairly constant at around 8000. The table below shows the number of flights and the average number of passengers arriving from within the UK, the European Community, the USA and countries outside these areas.

Time period	from UK	from EC	from USA	from others
0800–0900	2-220	0-0	1-130	0-0
0900–1000	5-560	1-120	2-320	1-200
1000–1100	3-280	3-350	0-0	0-0
1100–1200	3-250	2-310	0-0	0-0
1200–1300	2-190	2-240	0-0	1-220
1300–1400	1-150	1-120	0-0	0-0
1400–1500	2-200	0-0	0-0	0-0
1500–1600	3-310	2-180	0-0	1-200
1600–1700	4-360	2-180	0-0	0-0
1700–1800	5-410	2-190	0-0	0-0
1800–1900	6-500	2-150	0-0	1-190
1900–2000	3-330	1-140	1-140	0-0
2000–2100	2-180	1-120	2-300	2-270

Your tasks

1 Study the following questions. To what extent do you think they might affect the levels of customer care provided at Midshire Airport?

a) What fluctuations in the flow of incoming passengers are evident during the day?

b) What problems are created by the management specifying that Customs and Immigration staff work in continuous 8-hour shifts?

c) Would a split-shift system mean that a better service could be offered to the public?

2 The catering services at Midshire Airport are due for a complete overhaul. Draw up a list of general recommendations showing where you think the management should concentrate their main efforts in order to meet the likely needs of incoming passengers.

You should consider issues relating to time, personnel and types of cuisine.

3 A survey of incoming passengers has revealed the following statistics:
- 20 per cent of all arrivals would prefer to travel from the airport to the city of Midtown, some 15 minutes drive away, by taxi
- 50 per cent prefer the cheaper option of the half-hourly bus service (current capacity: 60 passengers)
- 30 per cent are either met by friends or relatives or have parked their own cars in nearby suburbs, as the airport does not as yet have a long stay car park.

Assume that on average two passengers travel in each taxi, the management is considering modifying the bus service timetable, and that funds have been promised to improve the car parking facilities. Draw up a plan to respond as far as possible to the customer needs as expressed in the survey.

6.2 Customer care: staff appearance

Develops knowledge and understanding of the following element:
6.1 Investigate customer service in leisure and tourism

Supports development of the following core skills:
Communication 3.2 (Task 1)
Communication 3.1, 3.3 (Task 2)

New leisure and tourism facilities have to decide how customers will be able to recognise company employees. First impressions are important, and the appearance of both staff coming into contact with customers and the facility itself will determine whether visitors leave with a positive impression.

If customers have doubts about the appearance of company employees, even if these are based on personal dislikes, it will be more difficult to win their trust – essential if the company is in the business of selling to them. Customers are, of course, individuals but many companies take the view that the majority may still dislike, for example, men wearing earrings or women in trousers and they may discourage these among their staff.

Uniforms have a number of potential advantages.
- They help customers to identify staff easily.
- They can be a means of marketing: the styles and colours can match the company logo and be emphasised in advertising and promotion.

35

A member of staff at a theme park in entertainment costume.

- If the design and materials are well chosen, a uniform can help boost morale and help to retain staff.

As most people will remember from schooldays, however, wearing a uniform does not automatically make people look smart, and telling someone else how they should look without giving offence requires sensitivity. Companies such as airlines, where a high standard of smartness is demanded, may give cabin staff very specific guidance about what make-up, hair styles and jewellery are acceptable. Similarly cleanliness is a sensitive but vital area for any company whose employees are in regular contact with customers: few of us wish to be served by someone who is dirty or smelly.

The appearance of the facility itself – whether it is a travel agency, a hotel room, or an attraction – is equally important. For example, if a travel agent's window contains only untidy handwritten lists of holiday offers, potential customers will go elsewhere. If it is dimly lit and the brochures are organised in such a way that it is difficult for people to find what they want, customers will not stay long. There may be very little floor space but half-empty coffee cups and ash trays full of old cigarette ends can easily be kept away from public areas. People often browse through brochures in a travel agency without returning them neatly to the proper rack. Attention to this and small details such as keeping the special offers advertised up-to-date can go a long way towards giving customers a good first impression.

Your tasks

1 Write a brief description of the different uniforms worn by three individuals you have seen working in leisure and tourism.

   a) How suitable were the outfits for the jobs they were doing?

   b) What impression did the clothes give you?

   c) Do you think the impact on you was what was intended?

   d) Are there any ways in which the uniform might not always create the effect the company intends?

2 The following people are key employees in new leisure and tourism ventures:
   - a woman carrying small posies of real and dried flowers in a basket to sell to tourists and theatre-goers in a city centre
   - a man, representing the British Tourist Authority at a series of trade fairs and exhibitions in Eastern Europe, with the job of encouraging people to visit Britain
   - the driver of a miniature railway which is to be installed at a model village attraction, where it will run around the perimeter

- a woman who is to act as guide at a country house newly open to the public which contains a famous art collection and also a maze of secret passages
- a female employee in a small new travel agency intending to specialise in tours of India and Pakistan.

a) What impressions do you think the employers of each of these five people would wish them to make on customers?

b) You are asked to design a uniform for each employee. In each case in which order would you place these three priorities:
  - durability
  - cost
  - appearance?

c) Suggest reasons in each case why some materials and colours would be more suitable than others.

6.3 Customers with special needs: wheelchair access

Develops knowledge and understanding of the following element:
6.1 Investigate customer service in leisure and tourism

Supports development of the following core skills:
Communication 3.4 (Task 1)
Communication 3.2 (Task 2)

The Holiday Care Service is a national charity which provides holiday information and support for disabled people, single parents, those on low incomes, carers and anyone else in need.

The Holiday Service joined with the four National Tourist Boards – in England, Wales, Scotland and Northern Ireland – in the Tourism for All campaign. One part of this campaign was the launch in 1990 of a system of identifying which types of accommodation provide access for wheelchair users and others who have difficulty walking.

The regional tourist boards put the places inspected into one of three categories. The system is applied not only to hotels and guest houses but also to self-catering apartments, camping and caravan sites and chalets. Crown, key and Q systems enable potential visitors to judge the general facilities and quality standards of accommodation they may be planning to use.

Inspected premises which reach the standards suggested by the Holiday Care Service may display an 'Accessible' symbol which will indicate the category they have been awarded.
- To achieve category 3 they must be accessible to a wheelchair user who is also able to walk a short distance and up at least three steps.
- Category 2 means the accommodation is also accessible to a wheelchair user with assistance.
- Category 1 means that the accommodation is accessible to a wheelchair user travelling alone.

The criteria used could have been stricter, but it was argued that this would have reduced the choice of places to stay to the very small number designed or adapted for easy and regular wheelchair use.

The criteria which have to be met before the 'Accessible' symbol can be displayed cover a number of areas.

- A public entrance must be accessible from a car park or setting down point.
- If the accommodation has a car park, a reservable space should be made available when required. This space should have a minimum width of 3.6 metres for Category 1.
- The route from the car park to the entrance should be free of obstacles, with no more than three steps for Category 3, and one step for Category 2.
- A level or ramped path must be available to qualify for Category 1.

There are a number of conditions laid down for the inside of all types of inspected accommodation.

- At least one bedroom and, where they are present, one lounge and one restaurant or dining room must be accessible to a wheelchair user.
- The top two categories (1 and 2) must have an accessible restaurant table with adequate space underneath for a wheelchair user to eat in comfort.
- There are minimum measurements for doorways, spaces beyond doors and corridors.
- The number of steps permissible within each category is the same inside the building as outside.
- Lifts must be large enough to hold a wheelchair, and for Category 1 automatic doors and controls must be within reach.
- Bedrooms and bathrooms require a number of specific conditions before they are approved by inspectors.
- There must be sufficient bedside space for a wheelchair user to transfer from wheelchair to bed and vice versa.
- Controls for television, lights, other switches and door handles and locks must be within reach.
- Bathrooms and toilets require good access and adequate space for manoeuvre.
- Suitable support rails are essential if any accommodation is to be placed in Category 1 or 2.

Your tasks

I Answer the following questions based on information given in the passage:

a) Why do you think the Tourism for All campaign was launched?

b) What difficulties might individual providers of tourist accommodation have if they wish to adapt their premises for wheelchair users?

c) Can you name any activities within holiday accommodation, but not mentioned in the passage, which wheelchair visitors might find easier if there is some special provision?

d) A large hotel is thinking of employing a wheelchair user. How do you think this might affect the hotel?

2 The 'Accessible' scheme is being extended so that it will cover fully self-catering accommodation and holiday caravan and camping parks.

Draw up a detailed list of criteria which could be used to award the three 'Accessible' symbols in each of the two following accommodation areas:
- the kitchens of self-catering apartments
- the layout of a camping and caravan site.

6.4 Customer care: price and quality

Develops knowledge and understanding of the following element:
6.2 Investigate sales and selling as part of customer service in leisure and tourism

Supports development of the following core skills:
Communication 3.1, 3.4 (Task 1)
Communication 3.1 (Task 2)
Communication 3.1 (Task 3)
Application of number 3.2; Communication 3.1, 3.4 (Task 4)

Leisure and tourism customers are not always buying a manufactured article, but they will still want value for money. More is expected from a holiday costing £1000 than from one costing half that sum. Golfers joining a club with exceptionally high fees expect the course to be in good condition and the clubhouse to be reasonably comfortable.

Price is a very easy way of measuring competing tourism and leisure services. Tour operators in particular have used price-cutting as an important way of attracting a larger share of the market. This both drastically reduced profit margins and allowed little leeway to protect the quality of the holidays they were offering. Some companies were forced out of business as a result. Another result was that many companies' holiday packages became difficult to distinguish from those offered by their competitors.

Customers are clearly not going to pay extra for a holiday which is identical to a less expensive one. They may, however, be reluctant to buy something which they see as cheap. Customers will feel this way if they think that the low price is a result of cheap materials, poor workmanship or inferior service and facilities. Tour operators also found that by concentrating on price they tended to move down-market. This meant that they had to attract a higher number of relatively low-spending customers to make a profit. Tour operators looking for a more reliable market concentrated on quality and charged a more realistic price, so that they had fewer customers but these paid more than people going on very cheap holidays. These companies reasoned that in difficult economic times the low-spending mass market is the first to disappear.

If companies want customers to believe that price is not the only important factor, their competing products have to have distinctive qualities. In the case of holidays this might be the actual destination choice or, if customers are booking a hotel, it might be the specific leisure facilities it has to offer. Products actually made in Britain are always going to find it difficult to compete on price terms alone with similar products made in parts of the world where labour costs are very much lower.

If the customer is going to receive value for money, it is vital that the seller is fully aware of the customer's needs. A travel agent may know that its customers want a holiday, but they must find out what the customer's own preferences and previous experience are if they are to provide value for money. Even with leisure and tourism the product needs to be properly designed. For example, customers renting a badminton court in a sports hall where the next court is being used for trampolining may feel this is poor planning.

Sellers should also be aiming for reliability, notoriously difficult in areas like travel where delays can be caused by events beyond the control of travel agents and tour operators themselves. Feedback from satisfied customers is critical if the reliability of something like individual holiday packages is to be established. As there is no manufactured product involved, this is the best way of gathering evidence for customers of the performance of what they are thinking of buying. A growing number of tour operators have improved the compensation they offer customers if their itineraries are disrupted. The European Community Travel Directive, launched on January 1st 1993, strengthens the **liability** of any company offering a tour package. Any company offering two elements from transport, accommodation, or other tourism services is made liable for any customer claims which arise from an accident, fatality or major disturbance affecting their booked package.

Maintaining a consistent service is essential if a company claims to offer value for money. A tour operator needs to be sure that a hotel can maintain its standards, regardless of any changes in staff or increases in occupancy rate. Forward planning is essential, particularly where maintenance or refurbishment is likely to disrupt normal business. Ideally such work should be done out of season, but operators in any case should inform customers of any unavoidable disruption.

Your tasks

The itineraries of three 1993 tours of India are given on pages 41 and 42. They were priced as follows.
● The Magic of India, from £745
● Images of India, from £1,213
● The Rajah, from £913

Working in pairs, adopt in turn the roles of travel agency counter staff and potential customers interested in touring India. You should prepare for this task by creating a number of profiles representing customers with different backgrounds, commitments and needs. You should also read the terms and conditions at the back of a tour operator's brochure offering tours to India, and establish the booking and payment procedures used by a local travel agent.

1 The travel counsellor should talk the customer through the features and main selling points of each tour.

2 The travel counsellor should discuss the relevance of each tour to the specific needs and interests identified in the client profiles.

3 The travel counsellor should provide answers to any questions the customer might have and seek to reassure them over any doubts.

4 The travel counsellor should explain the basic terms and conditions applying to a similar holiday tour, including booking, insurance and payment procedures.

THE MAGIC OF INDIA Escorted from Delhi back to Delhi

10 DAY TOUR

ITINERARY

1st Day Assemble at Heathrow for the British Airways flight to Delhi.

2nd day Early morning arrival in Delhi where your tour escort will meet you and take you to the Oberoi Maidens Hotel. The morning is free (to catch up on sleep or relax by the swimming pool). In the afternoon visit New Delhi, with its spacious wide roads and Lutyens-designed seat of government, originally built for the British Raj.

3rd day Morning tour of Old Delhi, the 17th century city called Shahjahanabad still reminiscent of Mogul times with its maze of alleys and bazaars dominated by the magnificent Red Fort and the marble domed Jama Masjid mosque. Afternoon free.

4th day Full morning's journey by road to Agra calling en route at Sikandra, burial place of Akbar the Great. Stay at the Clarks Shiraz Hotel. In the evening there may be an opportunity to visit the incomparable and romantic Taj Mahal by moonlight.

5th day Morning visit to the Mogul Red Fort and to the Taj Mahal by daylight, still beautiful but not so mysterious. Afternoon at leisure.

6th day We have a day travelling to Jaipur but calling en route at Fatehpur Sikri built by Akbar in AD 1575 and deserted after a few years though the magnificent Mogul buildings still remain intact. Travel on to Bharatpur, previously a royal hunting reserve but now a bird sanctuary. (This reserve will not be included from April to June.) In the afternoon continue to Jaipur and the Clarks Amer Hotel.

7th day In the morning we have a tour of this rose-red city visiting the Hawa Mahal (Palace of the Winds) and the Maharajah's Palace. Afternoon free.

8th day Visit Amber, The old city of Jaipur, and take an elephant ride to the Palace set on a hill dominating the town. We return to the Oberoi Maidens Hotel, Delhi in the afternoon.

9th day At leisure. Alternatively leave Delhi for one of our extension holidays.

10th day Early morning departure by British Airways for London, where we arrive at 1.00 p.m.

Meals: continental breakfast and dinner each day.

HOTELS

The hotels chosen for the Magic of India tour have been carefully selected and represent excellent value for money. All properties have full facilities., including pool and pleasant gardens, and are of medium standard. India is a thrilling experience, but the first-time visitor should allow differences in standards to those in Europe.

Images of India

India — a country of diverse cultures, architectures, peoples, landscapes, history, sights, sounds and mysteries. This tour offers a superb introduction, encompassing some of India's most fascinating and awe-inspiring attractions. Marvel at the splendour of Delhi's Red Fort, and at the intricate facade of Jaipur's fabled Palace of the Winds. Experience the spell-binding beauty of Agra's Taj Mahal, the famous erotic carvings at Khajuraho, and the intriguing city of Varnasi on the sacred waters of the Ganges. You also have the option of visiting Kathmandu in Nepal, in the foothills of the Himalayas, or the scenic lakeland of Srinagar in Kashmir.

9-night holiday – price includes Intercontinental flights on British Airways or Air India • Accommodation with private bathroom • Return airport to hotel transfers • Sightseeing as detailed • Services of Tour Escorts Days 2 to 10 • Jetset Luxury Travel Kit

ITINERARY

Departs – Sun
Hotel nights – Delhi 2, Jaipur 2, Agra 1, Khajuraho 1, Varanasi 1, Delhi 1.

Day 1 London/Delhi
Depart London Heathrow on British Airways or Air India.

Day 2 Delhi
Arrive in Delhi early this morning and transfer to the Taj Mahal hotel. Today is free to explore.

Day 3 Delhi
Morning at leisure. Your afternoon sightseeing tour of Old and New Delhi includes the Qurab Minar, Lakshminarayan Temple, Parliament House, the famous Red Fort and the beautiful Jama Masjid mosque.

Day 4 Delhi/Jaipur
This morning we drive to Jaipur. Visit the ancient hillside capital of Amber en route (which you approach on elephant back). Stay at the Rambagh Palace Hotel in Jaipur. Afternoon at leisure.

Day 5 Jaipur
Today you take a sightseeing tour of this magnificent pink city: visit the Maharaja's City Palace and its famous observatory, Jantar Mantar, and the Ram Niwas Gardens. Admire the Hawa Mahal, or Palace of the Winds, the fantastic soaring facade of pink stone.

Day 6 Jaipur/Agra
Depart for Agra, visiting the graceful red sandstone city of Fatehpur Sikri en route. On arrival in Agra transfer to the Taj View hotel. Afternoon at leisure.

Day 7 Agra
This morning visit the stunning Taj Mahal, built by the Moghul Emperor Shahjahan as a tomb for his queen. Later visit the Agra Fort with its many beautiful buildings, including the Pearl Mosque.

Day 8 Agra/Khajuraho
This afternoon fly to Khajuraho and the Chandela Hotel. Spend the rest of the day exploring Khajuraho.

Day 9 Khajuraho/Varanasi
In the morning visit the Khajuraho Temples, built by the Chandela Kings between AD 950 and 1050 and decorated with lavishly erotic Hindu sculptures. This afternoon fly to Varanasi; stay at the Taj Ganges.

Day 10 Varanasi/Delhi
An early morning drive through the city takes you to the riverbank for a boat ride on the holy river Ganges. See the bathing ghats, the pilgrims purifying themselves and the cremation sites. Then tour the many magnificent temples and palaces of Benaras city. In the evening fly back to Delhi where you stay at the Taj Mahal hotel.

Day 11 Delhi/London
Your early morning flight arrives in London around midday.

Meals – breakfast and dinner daily.

Local guide escort Days 2 to 10.

The Rajah
- Delhi
- Agra & Taj Mahal
- Jaipur

T*his short tour of the fascinating cities of Delhi, Agra and Jaipur, known as India's Golden Triangle, will show you the most popular sights of India, at a very attractive price. The hotels used are smaller and simpler than those featured on our more expensive arrangements, yet they offer a good standard of comfort and service, representing tremendous value for the budget conscious. We also offer a choice of extensions to Kashmir, Nepal, Goa or Thailand.*

Day 1 Fri London/Delhi
Depart Heathrow this evening by Air India flight to Delhi.
Day 2 Sat Delhi
On arrival in Delhi this morning, transfer to the Siddarth Hotel. The rest of the day is at leisure.
Day 3 Sun Delhi
During your time in Delhi, you are free to make your own discoveries in this imposing city. Perhaps take a tour of New Delhi, a city of wide avenues and imperial buildings, built by the British as the new capital of India early this century. Take a taxi to Janpath market and Connaught Place for the best shopping in Delhi or visit some of the many fascinating museums and beautiful parks which the city has to offer. Then visit Old Delhi, the city made rich and powerful by the Moghul emperors, including the huge Jama Masjid Mosque and Shah Jehan's magnificent Red Fort, Lal Qila, with its gardens, courtyards, palaces and halls. Or visit Chandni Chowk, meaning literally moonlit crossroads, and now probably the busiest street on earth. This evening why not see the Red Fort son et lumiere for a fascinating account of India's history, or a performance of Indian dances.
Day 4 Mon Delhi/Agra
Depart late this morning by air for Agra, for 2 nights at the Clarks Shiraz. Rest of the day at leisure. A late afternoon introductory visit to the Taj Mahal – the highlight of your trip – is recommended.
Day 5 Tue Agra
Day at leisure. This morning you are free to make a more leisurely tour of the Taj Mahal, India's most famous structure and often considered the world's most beautiful monument. Also try to see Itmad-ud-Daulah's smaller yet intricately decorated tomb and Agra Fort with its towering walls, marble mosques and palaces

Day 6 Wed Agra/Jaipur
Depart this morning by road for Jaipur. Transportation will be air conditioned on all departures between March and October. En route you will visit the deserted Moghul city of Fatehpur Sikri, built by Akbar in 1569. Arrive at your hotel, the Clarks Amer, in the afternoon, and the rest of the day is at leisure. Why not take an afternoon sightseeing tour of the beautiful walled 18th century city of Jaipur, visiting the Maharajah's Palace, Jantar Mantar – the 17th century observatory, the Central Museum of the Albert Hall and Ram Nivas Gardens.
Day 7 Thu Jaipur
A further day at leisure. We suggest an optional morning drive to see the delicately carved Palace of the Winds, then on to Amber, once capital of the Rajput Empire, to ride regally to the hilltop fortress on an elephant's back. At Amber Fort, see the Sheesh Mahal, (Hall of Mirrors) and the Jai Mandir (Hall of Victory). You can visit the white marble Sila Devi Temple with its clanging bells and drums. Spend the afternoon either relaxing at your hotel or exploring the city further, perhaps visiting its colourful bazaars and markets – Jaipur is well known for its gem cutting, brassware and Rajasthani cotton printing.
Day 8 Fri Jaipur/Delhi
About midday fly to Delhi and the Siddarth Hotel, before your transfer to the airport later tonight.
Day 9 Sat Delhi/London
A very early morning Air India flight to Heathrow, arriving this morning.

Note: It may sometimes be necessary to use hotels other than those stated.

6.5 Sales promotion: selling Scotland to America

Develops knowledge and understanding of the following element:
6.2 Investigate sales and selling as part of customer service in leisure and tourism

Supports development of the following core skills:
Communication 3.2, 3.4 (Task 1)
Application of numner 3.1, Communication 3.1 (Task 2)
Communication 3.2, 3.3; Information Technology 3.1, 3.2, 3.3 (Task 3)
Communication 3.1, 3.2 (Task 4)

The main purpose of most marketing activities is to increase sales volume and to meet revenue targets. Yet before any sale can be made, the attention of the buyer has to be gained. Often this is done by advertising, but it may also be achieved through sales promotion. There are many different kinds of sales promotion, but they are all intended to have an immediate effect on sales volume.

The main difficulty in promoting sales in leisure and tourism often arises from the nature of the product. If the customer simply wants a hotel room for the night, the sale is likely to be transacted directly with the customer. In other words enquiries, reservation requirements and booking will be handled by communication between the customer and hotel reception staff. Other tourism products, like holidays, are too complex and too expensive to be sold without an often lengthy process of analysing different products to see which meets all the customer's various needs. It is more difficult to decide exactly what is being sold – is it the destination or the accommodation, or the climate or a combination of a whole variety of ingredients? When all these factors are involved, it is fairly easy to see that it is not a simple matter to sell a destination to an individual customer.

So, if selling a destination to an individual customer is difficult, how can a destination be sold and what sort of people might be interested in doing this? Perhaps the most common method is to try and sell the destination to the travel trade, and persuade them that, as a product, it has more to offer than its competitors. There are a number of ways the destination can put itself in a favourable light with those who sell holidays direct to the public, such as travel agents. Incentives can be offered if agreed sales targets for the destination are reached. Educational visits are often made available by destinations, both to key travel agency personnel and to travel journalists. One common method of promoting destinations is through special events, generally including a major presentation, to publicise the production of a new brochure featuring the destination and its attractions. This will include participation in trade fairs and exhibitions.

This kind of promotional event may be mounted by a number of different local interests. Regional tourist boards are often involved. Local councils may provide support. However the majority of the funding and planning is likely to come from those with most to gain from increases in tourism in the destination, namely the major hotel groups, tour operators, transport companies and attraction owners operating in the area. Whoever organises the event, the most important factor in their planning is targeting a market that the destination will appeal to and ensuring that this market is well represented in the audience. For example, destinations wishing for more overseas tourists to purchase holidays in their region will have to target directly a range of different companies and organisations in a country which either already sends substantial numbers of visitors or where there is evidence that many could be persuaded to try the destination in question.

One method by which a destination can attract more overseas sales is through a carefully organised sales trip to a country which is regarded as an important market for inbound tourism. For example, a consortium of Scottish hotel owners, calling themselves Scottish Connoisseurs and representing six of Scotland's most luxurious hotels, undertook a sales trip to North America in 1994. Much was

Scottish scenery – the harbour at Tobermory, Mull.

already known about American attitudes to overseas travel. The US is Scotland's main source of foreign visitors. They are attracted by the culture and heritage, as well as the common language. The most popular activities which they take part in are visiting historic houses, cathedrals, museums and art galleries; shopping and visiting the theatre; touring the countryside; sightseeing. This knowledge was crucial in planning how to present the product, in this case Scotland, to them.

Before they could decide what they wanted to say about Scotland, the organisers of the trip had to be sure that they would be talking to the right people. It would be of no benefit to make a brilliant presentation to people who were not in a position to influence sales. A number of groups were identified as being important, including:

- American travel agents specialising in the luxury end of the UK market;
- travel journalists writing for newspapers and magazines traditionally read by high spenders;
- high-spending groups like American Express Platinum card holders.

Given that the group had only 12 days in which to make an impact, they also had to choose which cities might provide the most responsive audiences. Scottish Connoisseurs targeted four main cities which generate significant numbers of outbound tourists – New York, Atlanta, San Francisco and Los Angeles.

Though the trip was obviously expected to generate revenue through increased bookings, its costs clearly had to be met before any of this expected income was received. Funding came through a number of sources. Approximately two-thirds was provided by the individual members of the consortium themselves. The remainder came through sponsorship and a contribution from the British Tourist Authority. The sponsors had clear Scottish connections and benefited from being featured in the consortium's brochure, and from the presence of some of their products, such as spring water and malt whisky, at lunches and presentations. The British Tourist Authority made a financial contribution, supporting its main objective of marketing Britain overseas.

There are many costs built into an overseas sales trip of this sort, apart from the travel and accommodation expenses of the participants. Many of the groups which the team needs to impress – including travel journalists, upmarket travel agents and high-spending groups like American Express Platinum card holders – are unlikely to respond positively to a travel lecture in modest surroundings. They will expect top quality catering, an interesting presentation, individual advice and attention, and a pleasant, comfortable environment.

Funds also had to be invested in producing a brochure for the trip. A public relations officer, based in New York, and therefore with good American contacts, was also paid a fee in return for co-ordinating local arrangements and ensuring the presence of influential media figures at the group's presentations. Having a good local contact was important in issuing invitations and collating replies. The consortium paid for several people to go with them. Two musicians travelled with the group, providing a flavour of Scottish culture through their playing of bagpipes, fiddle and accordion music. Dr Michael Shea, the Queen's former press secretary, accompanied them, his high profile enabling them to make useful contacts. He also wrote the introduction to the brochure.

If the various audiences for the sales trip were right, the message they were to receive had to be appropriate too. The main focus of presentations was considered vital to the trip's success. They could not afford to confuse potential customers with too much detail, but at the same time had to get across a message about the individual character of Scotland as a destination. The Scottish Connoisseurs stressed the 'authenticity' of what Scotland had to offer, and in particular its distinctive culture, its spectacular scenery, its good food and the fact that it was the home of golf. The selling of individual hotels of members of the consortium depended to a great extent on the personal contact established over lunches and dinners, once formal presentations had been completed.

The use of presentations as a sales tool is common. Travel agents and journalists who are very familiar with the medium may be hard to please. Decisions have to be taken about whether to go for something unusual and unexpected, which runs the risk of appearing gimmicky, or settling for a more straightforward approach. The Scottish Connoisseurs, wishing to emphasise authenticity, developed their presentation as an audio-visual show, presenting striking images of lakes, golf courses, castles, heather and mountains. The commentary and accompanying music stressed the themes of culture, landscape, tradition, and high standards of food and accommodation. These events require meticulous planning, to ensure that the quality of personal service, catering, comfort and technical backup is of the highest quality. These factors may be as important as the destination itself in determining how individual audience members react to the event.

The real test of the value of a sales trip such as this comes in assessing the subsequent bookings which are made from the targeted market. For the trip to be worth while, these bookings need to generate more revenue than the costs to each consortium member of putting the trip together. However, it may take two or three years for individual hotels in the consortium to establish the number of additional bookings the trip generated and to determine which event or presentation was directly responsible for each extra sale.

Your tasks

1 Choose either an existing tourist destination in your region or a location which has the potential to attract visitors from outside the region.

   Identify the main characteristics which attract visitors currently or which could be exploited in the future development of tourism.

2 Identify a market group outside the region and explain why you think it might be a particularly appropriate group to target in an attempt to increase the number of visits from outside the region.

3 Prepare a presentation to be given in the region of your target market, aimed at directly increasing sales of holidays to your chosen destination.

4 Choose small groups to represent members of the audience invited to your presentation, e.g. local travel agents, journalists from local newspapers and magazines, local radio and television personnel, consumer groups.

   Each of these groups should listen to a selection of your presentations and prepare and ask a number of questions to test whether or not they are convinced they should give their support to selling the destination.

6.6 Customer service at a motorway service station

Develops knowledge and understanding of the following element:
6.1 Investigate customer service in leisure and tourism

Supports development of the following core skills:
Communication 3.1 (Task 1)
Application of number 3.1; Communication 3.2; Information Technology 3.1, 3.3 (Task 2)
Communication 3.2 (Task 3)

Toddington Motorway Service Station lies on the M1, some 30 miles north of London. It was built in 1964, making it the second oldest motorway service station in Britain. It lies on one of the busiest stretches of motorway in the country, carrying a high volume of commercial and private traffic heading to and from London and the Channel ports. The completion of the M25 has increased traffic heading to and from the other main motorway routes to the south and west, such as the M3 and the M4.

The range of services offered to customers is partly controlled by regulations. Unlike a shop or a suburban petrol station Toddington is required by the Department of Transport to meet certain conditions in order to continue operating. It must offer a 24-hour fuel service, and parking and toilet facilities must be constantly available. The parking space must accommodate cars, coaches and heavy goods vehicles. Some form of food provision must also be available, but the service station does not have to keep restaurants open all night.

Apart from fuel, Toddington provides three main types of service.

- *Food services* – these include an all-day breakfast service, light snacks, hot meals and drinks. They may be obtained in a restaurant, a fast food outlet, from takeaway kiosks or from vending machines.
- *Retail services* – these include the sale of newspapers, sweets, a large variety of snacks, cigarettes and some souvenirs.
- *Accommodation services* – overnight accommodation is provided in lodges with adjacent car parking space. Granada, the company which operates Toddington, began to put lodges on motorway service stations in 1988.

Like most of the bigger motorway service stations Toddington is a double-sided site, with all facilities on the north-bound side of the motorway exactly matching those on the south except for the lodges, all on the south side. Smaller stations may have all their facilities on one side of the motorway with a pedestrian footbridge connecting the two, or even as on the M6 north of Preston, be confined solely to one side.

Granada believes that branding is important in building up customer loyalty, and hence the design and layout of the facilities on each side is identical. However, in practice the customer needs of those stopping on the different sides of the M1 are often different. Those heading south are often going to London and are therefore nearly at their destination. If they stop they may well only do so to use the toilet facilities which will bring Granada no revenue at all. More north-bound travellers stop for a full meal. Coaches coming off the Channel ferries will often be approaching three hours' driving time by the time they reach Toddington and the drivers will be required to take a break. All of these factors mean that, despite the similar facilities, the spend on the north-bound side at Toddington is significantly greater than that on the south-bound side.

Customers using facilities like Toddington expect a fairly rapid service. One of the key factors in managing a motorway service station successfully is the ability to predict busy periods and to react to them quickly. Sometimes this is relatively easy. If a team from the north or Midlands is playing in the FA Cup Final at Wembley then Toddington is certain to have a busy time on the Saturday morning. A major pop concert or a holiday weekend can have similar effects. Whenever there is a sudden influx of customers it is important that there are enough staff immediately available to handle their needs quickly and efficiently. The manager of a motorway service station will also be aware of local traffic conditions. Though major motorway traffic jams might appear to provide lots of customers eager to leave the motorway for a break, in practice they are often then in a hurry and short of patience, and so may not make ideal customers.

Toddington needs 350 staff in order to provide the services it offers. Approximately 60 per cent of these are full-time. Unlike most high street outlets, the fast food takeaway service and the retail areas stay open until 10 p.m. and 11 p.m. respectively. Part-time workers were originally taken on to cover weekend work but they are now also used to cover the extended evening hours needed. In addition to staff to operate retail, catering, lodges and the forecourts, Toddington also has to employ cleaners and drivers. The drivers are needed because the location of the service station means that employees without their own transport would be unable to get to work by public transport.

Most employees will work one of two main shifts: 7 a.m. to 3 p.m. or 3 p.m. to 11 p.m. However, office staff and part-time staff may also require transport at other times. Staff are recruited from an area taking in Bedford, Dunstable, Luton and various villages in between. Travel-to-work time in the company bus can be up to an hour, as each round trip may have to take in many pick-up points. Providing customer service over such long time periods is a factor which ordinary food outlets do not generally have to contend with.

New employees go through an induction programme showing them what levels of service are expected. The programme covers essential issues to do with health and safety, food hygiene and emergency procedures. Progress through a training programme developed by Granada is recorded by means of flags of achievement.

To be financially successful a motorway service station has to be aware of what customers want. Most research suggests that those travelling by road have two major priorities:

- *value for money* – they will compare the quality, quantity and price with other similar stopping places
- *good service* – they are aware of the speed, accuracy and politeness of the staff who serve them.

The needs of customers are monitored through research. Comment cards are placed near checkouts, asking customers to respond by ticking boxes indicating their view of the levels of service they received. They can either place these in a box or post them direct. The branding of all Granada's service stations is intended to send a message to all customers that, if they have enjoyed a break at one of the company's outlets, they will meet the same standards and facilities at any other. Special offers are used to promote the idea of value for money. These might include a special set-price breakfast including a number of items or an inclusive price for a dish of the day.

Customers may question the prices at motorway service stations, and they may often be higher than those elsewhere. A suburban supermarket is certain to offer lower petrol prices and high street food outlets may be less expensive. However, motorway service station costs are higher, largely as a result of having to provide a 24-hour service. Deregulation means that some new service stations may be allowed to operate on a more flexible basis and the existing stations will be keen to monitor the implications of this as they become clearer. Their main competition is still other motorway service stations, since it is only a minority of motorists who will leave the motorway in search of fuel or food.

A site like Toddington would expect to continue to attract a regular flow of customers, not least because of its strategic position. However, the operation has to achieve satisfactory financial and quality performances to maintain its position. Financial targets are set through budgets while all services are subject to audits which check their standards very precisely. A catering audit, for example, would check specifications, hygiene, portions and temperatures of food.

Your tasks

1 Arrange a visit to a motorway service station or roadside catering and/or accommodation outlet in your locality.

2 Devise a short survey which would enable you to collect data on the following:
- the volume of passing traffic
- the proportion of traffic which stops at the outlet
- the number and type of passengers in each stopping vehicle
- the actual use made of the facility by visitors.

3 Write a brief description of the range of services provided by the facility and the extent to which each meets the needs of the customers who use it.

6.7 Constructing customer questionnaires

Develops knowledge and understanding of the following element:
6.3 Analyse customer service quality for selected leisure and tourism organisations

Supports development of the following core skills:
Application of number 3.3 (Task 1)
Application of number 3.3; Communication 3.2 (Task 2)

Imagine that you have taken your family out for the day to a museum. There has been plenty to see, a lot of excitement and activity for the children and a great deal of walking. You are on your way out when a member of the museum staff presents you with a questionnaire with over twenty detailed answers to fill in. It is not surprising that many such questionnaires finish up in the wastepaper bin outside the main exit!

Overcoming people's reluctance is the first problem faced by the designer of a visitor questionnaire. Even where the questions are well thought out, if the visitors feel that the task is an unnecessary burden, the answers may not give a fair reflection of their attitudes. Visitors may be asked to fill in the forms at home and put them in the post, but this tends to reduce the percentage which are actually completed and returned.

The request to provide information has to be politely phrased, with a brief explanation about why the information is needed. The Museum of East Anglian Life, for example, heads its customer questionnaire with the following words:

> Before you leave the museum today, we would be most grateful if you would take the time to fill in this short questionnaire. We need to know what our visitors think so that we can continue to develop and improve the Museum and the facilities provided.

The time it takes respondents to complete the questionnaire will also affect the numbers who take the trouble to do so. The questions asked can be structured so that many of the answers only require a box to be ticked. Long or complicated questions should be avoided. Sometimes more descriptive answers may be necessary, particularly if the museum would like a range of suggestions. For example, a museum might want to ask visitors whether they had any suggestions for improvements which could be made to the facilities or services.

The actual content of the questions depends on what the devisers of the questionnaire think they need to know. They may think it is important to establish where their visitors come from. If they ask 'Where do you live?', they will collect a list of names of towns and villages which they will then have to categorise before the information tells them anything useful. If the question is phrased so that respondents have to choose from a range of options which list towns or regions, less analysis will be necessary.

Some questions will have an obvious marketing purpose. Finding out where the majority of visitors are staying will provide information about the best places to distribute publicity leaflets. Questions about who was in the visiting group, or about where they first heard of the place they are visiting will also generate data useful to the marketing department.

If the museum wants information to help to improve customer care the type of question required needs judgement and evaluation from the respondent. Care has to be taken with the wording of such questions, since it is very easy to phrase them suggesting a positive (Was the length of the queues acceptable?) or negative view ('Did you find the queues a nuisance?').

There are a number of ways in which customers can be asked to evaluate what they have seen and done.

- They can be asked to identify the best and worst: this enables a quick answer but allows for no explanation and may only draw responses about a limited number of features.
- Customers can be asked to rank features or exhibits in order of preference: this does not require much writing, but is not a very precise kind of evaluation, particularly if the list of features is long.
- The most common practice is to ask respondents to rate features on a five-point scale: very good, good, average, poor or very poor. This is still far from exact, but it does generate a general view about individual features without taking too much time to complete or analyse.

Some elements of customer care may be considered sufficiently important to have specific attention drawn to them:

- directional signs
- guides and information services
- facilities for children, the disabled or non-English speakers.

Finally, the deviser of the questionnaire tends to control what the customer is able to say, and the scope of the questions may give the respondent no chance of recording an important opinion, either constructive or critical. So most visitor surveys will end with an open invitation to comment or suggest improvements. Although these responses may be difficult to analyse, comments in response to this type of question are often the most useful in producing ideas for improving future customer care.

Your tasks

1 Analyse the feedback data gathered from visitor questionnaires at the Elthorne-on-Sea Toy and Games Museum.

Elthorne-on-Sea Toy and Games Museum: summary of selected responses to visitor questionnaires

562 responses were received, though not all respondents answered all questions.

Question 3 — **Are you staying away from where you live?**
Yes: 415 — No: 147

Question 4(a) — **If you are, are you staying in:**
Elthorne-on-Sea: 334 — Hanstone: 31
Much Ferndon: 19 — Lesser Ferndon: 4
others: 27

Question 4(b) — **Is your accommodation:**
Hotel: 67 — Guest house: 114
Camping: 130 — Self-catering: 66
Staying with friends: 38

Question 8 — **Where did you first hear about the museum?**
Tourist information centre: 98 — Leaflet: 137
Newspaper adverts: 191 — Local radio: 18
Signposts: 31 — From friends/locals: 87

Question 11(a) — **Which exhibit interested you most?**
The top 3 were:
Lady Hanstone's Dolls' House: 144 — The World of Victorian Board Games: 67
The Japanese Puppet Show: 105

Question 11(b) — **Which exhibit interested you least?**
The 3 most frequently mentioned were:
Needlework Through the Ages: 97 — The Rules of Playground Games: 73
The Spinning Top Exhibition: 74

Question 12 — **What other attractions do you think the museum should feature?**
The 3 most frequently mentioned were:
Computer games: 196 — Football: 54
More activities/things to do: 117

Question 13(a) — **Did you use the following at the museum?**
Free leaflet: 499 — Guide book: 118
Directional signs: 369

Question 13(b) — **How helpful did you find them?**

	very good	good	average	poor	very poor
Leaflet	151	195	107	39	7
Guide book	41	51	14	11	1
Directional signs	21	70	149	106	56

Question 14	**How would you rate the following ?**				
		very good	good	average	poor	very poor
	Staff	175	188	118	67	14
	Shop	58	104	172	98	70
	Parking facilities	11	44	125	108	63
	Labelling of exhibits	197	136	175	44	10

Question 15 — **What other suggestions for facilities or services do you have ?**
The 5 most frequently mentioned were:
Snack bar/catering outlet: 172
More modern games and toys: 91
More activities/trying things out: 66

Larger car park: 47
Leaflets/guide books designed for children: 29

2 What recommendations would you make for improving customer care and the products and services at the Museum?

6.8 American Express (Travel-Related Services division): evaluating customer care

Develops knowledge and understanding of the following element:
6.3 Analyse customer service quality for selected leisure and tourism organisations

Supports development of the following core skills:
Communication 3.2, 3.4 (Task 1)
Application of number 3.1; Communication 3.2; Information Technology 3.1, 3.4 (Task 2)

In addition to its well known financial operations American Express is a major provider of **retail travel**. The company has always stressed the quality of the service it provides. The values of the company (known internally as Blue Box values, after the company logo) are

American Express is a major provider of retail travel.

based on principles which emphasise integrity, teamwork, quality, community and, above all, the importance of the customer. This means that providing an outstanding service to customers is fundamental to the way the company's business is planned and run.

Evaluating customer care accurately requires the establishment of standards against which performance can be measured. Some of these standards may be measurable, for example the time it takes to answer telephone enquiries, while others, like the way face-to-face customers are greeted, may be more difficult to quantify. Nevertheless the skill of greeting customers correctly can be broken down into a number of basic requirements. American Express employees are expected to:

- make eye contact
- smile when greeting the customer
- use their name when it is known
- ask open questions with enthusiasm.

Targets can be set for telephone answering. These will generally take account of past experience to set a percentage of calls which should be answered within ten seconds of being received. A target may also be set showing the maximum percentage acceptable for calls where the caller hangs up or is lost in transfer. One way of evaluating the quality of the answers given to customers on the telephone is to suggest standard formats for the most common types of enquiry. This is often a matter of identifying appropriate information and recording it. Some companies use a **pro forma** which acts as a prompt to sales staff and ensures that they include all relevant details. American Express includes in its quality standard for answering the telephone correctly a requirement that important information is recapped at the end of the call.

Some elements of customer care seem too obvious to need stating, but they can still be overlooked. Anyone who comes into a travel agency to browse, for example, should be offered assistance. The majority will want some attention and advice, even if this is in their own time. An exchange of information is important even when a sale is not made immediately, since it may help to provide a more prompt and efficient service if the customer returns.

With more complicated sales, such as business or leisure travel, **documentation** will provide further evidence of the quality of customer care. It should be comprehensible, complete and provided sufficiently in advance of departure. Any special conditions or amendments should be clearly understood. American Express produces a check list for the documentation to be sent out to customers who have made travel reservations with them. A company quality standard states that 100% of such documentation should be complete and accurate. Weekly checks are carried out to monitor how consistently this standard is being achieved. The final travel tickets and details have to be delivered within an agreed time limit.

Any company seeking to provide an above-average service to customers will probably aim to add features which the customer is likely to see as extras. Airlines, for example, have frequently offered free gifts such as wash bags to first class passengers. American Express offers a range of additional information to travellers, while guides, gifts or complimentary foreign currency are offered to higher spenders.

Handling complaints is an important part of customer care. American Express argues that complaining customers are valuable in that they enable the company to put things right. If the complaint is dealt with promptly and in a constructive manner, the loyalty of the customer to the company can still be established. Early acknowledgement of the complaint and on-going information about progress in dealing with it are indications of good quality service. Wherever possible the response should be personal and not simply a standard form.

Your tasks

1 A local travel agency, Pip's Trips Limited, has circulated a questionnaire to its customers. A question about the quality of service provided resulted in the following responses:

   a) 'When I came in all the reps were busy, so I sat down to wait. Just as someone got up to go another customer came through the door and the rep served them, ignoring my presence altogether . . .'

   b) 'The phone always seemed to be engaged when I rang. I did try in the evenings but all I got was the answer phone. I didn't leave a message because I'm hard to contact at work . . .'

   c) 'When I insisted I wanted to go to Karpathos, because my mate had been there, the rep tried to argue. The place was nothing like I thought it would be. There was no night life at all, no proper lager, and the old folk on the beach kept wanting the ghetto blaster turned down. The whole thing was a waste of money and if you expect me to book with you again, I reckon you ought to provide me with a refund . . .'

   d) 'I eventually received excellent advice on what was a very complicated journey, but I found the long queue very frustrating . . .'

   e) 'I spoke to one rep on the phone and gave details of the type of holiday I wanted. I was told that they would have to check availability and would get back to me. When this didn't happen I rang again, to be told that the particular destination I had asked for was unreachable at the time of year I wanted to go . . .'

   f) 'I went into the office to explain that I was far from happy with the hotel we had been booked into. The rep was very abrupt, saying that this was not your responsibility and that I should write to the tour operator.'

   Write a letter from Philip Pirrip, Managing Director of Pip's Trips, to each of the customers, acknowledging their complaints and indicating how the company intends to respond.

2 Draw up a scheme which will enable Pip's Trips Limited to assess the way it handles customer complaints. The scheme should indicate the following:
   ● guidelines for staff initially handling complaints
   ● criteria for staff investigating complaints
   ● methods of collecting data about complaints from customers
   ● methods of analysing and reporting the data collected
   ● agreed style and content of responses to complaints.

6.9 Plan a customer service programme

Develops knowledge and understanding of the following element:
6.3 Analyse customer service quality for selected leisure and tourism organisations

Supports development of the following core skills:
Application of number 3.1; Communication 3.2; Information Technology 3.1, 3.3 (Task 1)
Communication 3.2 (Task 2)
Application of number 3.1; Communication 3.2; Information Technology 3.1, 3.3 (Task 3)
Communication 3.2, 3.3 (Task 4)

John Cameron arrived at the City Lodge Hotel on his first day as general manager. During his selection he had stayed at the hotel as a mystery guest so that he could experience for himself the standard of service the hotel offered.

The 3-star City Lodge Hotel was built in 1970 and, with 120 bedrooms all with private facilities, competes with many similar hotels in the area. The main business comes from conference delegates using the hotel's conference facilities and business travellers visiting companies in the business park close to the city. The hotel also attracts weekend visitors to the historical sites in the city and surrounding areas. Much of the weekend business comes from a coach tour company bringing 30 to 40 guests at any one time.

The hotel's occupancy rate for the last 12 months has been running at 60 per cent.

The hotel has 70 full-time and part-time staff, many of whom have worked at the hotel for some time.

During his stay as a mystery guest John made notes on the way that the hotel was operating so that, on taking up his appointment as general manager, he could discuss them with his management team.

He noted the following matters of concern:

- on making a call to the hotel the phone rang for 12 rings before being answered
- a newspaper requested the night before was not delivered
- he was told by reception that last orders in the restaurant were at 11.00 p.m. when in fact they were at 10.30 p.m.
- he was seated in the no smoking section of the restaurant and a person on the next table was smoking
- the starter he ordered took 25 minutes to arrive. The waiter commented that the delay was caused by the kitchen being slow that night
- when he requested some toothpaste he was directed to the shops five minutes' walk from the hotel
- room service breakfast ordered for 7 a.m. arrived at 7.20 a.m.
- the waiter bringing his breakfast tray did not knock on the door and did not speak while in the room
- when he checked out, the receptionist failed to make eye contact and seemed more concerned with talking to her colleague.

During his first week in his new position, John met with his heads of department. During the meeting he asked for details of any problems experienced in their departments. All replies referred to the lack of facilities and areas in need of refurbishment. None of the managers identified customer service as a concern.

On further investigation John found that on average four complaint letters arrived each week. He also noted that the duty manager's log book contained details of verbal complaints received.

At the first heads of departments meeting he presented an agenda item on the subject of customer service.

He posed the following question to his team:

'How do we know what level of service we are offering our customers?'

Derek, the chef, was the first to respond: 'If you're talking about customers, perhaps you don't need me. . . '

'On the contrary,' said John, 'you are a key member of the management team and this is a concern for all of us. I see customer service as a chain within the hotel and one that concerns us all. Remember, without the customer we would not be here. If we can improve customer service we will make a successful business and this will benefit us all.'

John went on to present what he saw as the hotel's key customer service activities:
1 providing information
2 selling and taking orders
3 presentation
4 settling terms of payment and credit arrangements
5 complaint handling.

He pointed out that many of these activities concerned all staff working in the hotel. Yet staff would naturally find some situations difficult to handle and therefore training was required to enable staff to deal with guests in a confident manner.

He highlighted the importance of product knowledge as a good starting point, using as an example the incident with reception giving him the wrong 'last orders' time when he stayed as a mystery guest.

He asked the group to discuss what information all staff need to know. He then left the room to organise some refreshments. On his return he noticed a list written on the flip chart.

Points included:
- opening and closing times
- laundry arrangements
- menu details
- details of local facilities, e.g. car parking
- check out and check in times.

At the end of the meeting he asked all managers to compile a list of ways to assess customer satisfaction in their departments. He also asked for ideas on how to monitor customer service.

At his next meeting, one week later, each member provided feedback to the group. Their ideas were summed up in the notes they had prepared.

Department	Suggestions for monitoring customer satisfaction
Front office	– number of discrepancies on guests' bills – amount of money deducted from bills as a result of complaints – number of guests returning – feedback from guests/companies who have stopped using the hotel – number of rings before a phone is answered
Restaurant/room service	– number of complaints/comments – time taken to deliver guests' orders – level of gratuities received from guests – number of meals served – number of diners returning
Housekeeping	– number of complaints/comments regarding rooms – number and nature of requests for extra items in rooms – time taken to deliver items requested
Kitchen	– time taken to prepare items after receiving orders – amount of food left on guests' plates – comments from guests
Accounts	– number of discrepancies on guests' accounts – number of bills with adjustments – feedback from guests when dealing with accounts queries
Maintenance	– number of rooms unable to be let at the end of a shift – time taken to complete maintenance tasks – comments from guests and other departments

John was pleased both by the points raised and by the amount of thought his team had given this.

He asked that all departments should keep a daily book in which they would record all customer service issues they had encountered. He also emphasised the need to observe the levels of service actually being offered more closely, and to make notes about inadequacies and suggestions for improvement.

He finished his meeting by introducing some key customer service standards:

1 all phones should be answered within 5 rings
2 all staff must wear uniform and a name badge
3 all messages received must be delivered within 10 minutes
4 all room service orders must be delivered within 30 minutes of receiving the order and within 10 minutes if it is a breakfast order
5 when known, all guests' surnames must be used
6 an order must be taken from a restaurant guest within 5 minutes of their being seated.

Your tasks

1 Compile a customer service questionnaire which would be placed in all the City Lodge Hotel's bedrooms. How would you encourage guests to complete the form?

2 Write a letter of welcome from the new general manager of the City Lodge Hotel to guests introducing him or herself and encouraging them to comment on the level of service they receive.

3 Design a product knowledge questionnaire that would help all hotel staff to give a higher standard of information about the hotel's services to guests.

4 Design a hand-out for staff, outlining the standards of personal and work area appearance required at the hotel.

6.10 Customer care techniques

Develops knowledge and understanding of the following element:
6.4 Deliver and evaluate customer service in leisure and tourism organisations

Supports development of the following core skills:
Communication 3.1, 3.4 (Task 1)
Communication 3.2 (Task 2)

As its name suggests, customer care is about looking after customers and making sure that they feel they have benefited from contact with company employees. The leisure and tourism industry, as a service industry, is highly dependent on successful customer care. Customers often have high expectations of pleasure from holiday and leisure activity and will naturally resent any employee who appears not to be living up to these expectations.

Providing good customer care is often a matter of communication. This can only happen if the customer regards the employee as approachable in the first place. A smart appearance, an observant outlook and being willing to take the initiative in asking if help is needed can all make the customer feel more at ease.

Even when contact has been made, the customer will gain little benefit if the employee is poorly informed. An employee in a travel agency will need to have a wide knowledge of holiday destinations, but customers may also want to know about insurance details, special travel arrangements, fare supplements or luggage allowances.

Contact between customers and employees, as between any strangers, can be affected by several factors. The employee has to judge quickly what the customer's needs are and has to be a good listener to do this effectively. He or she may have to prompt the customer with questions, while at the same time trying to make sure that they don't interrupt. There may be alternative solutions and customers are entitled to know what the choices are. Providing extra information in the form of leaflets, maps, addresses or brochures often helps to meet customer needs.

Telephone sales staff at work.

If the situation is complex, making notes may help. It can also be reassuring to both parties if the employee summarises what has been agreed at the end of the conversation. There are bound to be circumstances where an employee does not know all the answers. Rather than making up something, it is always better either to refer customers directly to someone who will know or to offer to provide information at a later time.

Not all customer contact is face to face. In leisure and tourism enquiries and reservations are often made by telephone. This often has the advantage of convenience, but it means the customer is less able to get an immediate feeling for the employee's manner and personality. This makes it essential for the employee to identify themselves at the beginning of the conversation.

Businesses which are highly dependent on telephone sales may wish to keep calls within a reasonable time limit. In sales or reservations departments they may encourage the use of standard forms prompting the employee to ask a number of structured questions. In a company selling business travel this ensures that all essential information for making a reservation is given. Good customer care, however, means that the employee could depart from this 'script' if the customer wished to add an extra question. The employee would also need to be surrounded by sufficient sources of reference to be able to answer it.

Whatever the type of communication, politeness is always preferable to indifference or rudeness. Leaving customers waiting on the end of a telephone line without explaining the reason for the delay will cause irritation. Failing to acknowledge the presence of other customers while you talk at length to a customer or other member of staff will have a similar effect. Telling people, without apology, that there is nothing that can be done about their enquiry or concern is also unlikely to encourage them to return.

There may be occasions when employees are faced with giving customers some unpleasant information. They may not be entitled to a refund, their accommodation may have been changed or the time of their flight may have been delayed. Generally it is advisable to be honest about the causes of the problem. It may be necessary to explain company policy on the issue and to show the reasons for this policy rather than, for example, simply telling them that they have totally misread the small print in a brochure!

Your tasks

1 Read the following opening remarks made in response to enquiries or questions from customers. How effective do you think they are?

a) I'm afraid we've made a right mess of this booking, sir . . .

b) I think it's somewhere near the town centre . . .

c) You can't really expect us to pay compensation for flight delays – that's the airline's responsibility . . .

d) I'm very sorry, madam, but as you can see we're exceptionally busy this evening. I'll certainly do everything I can to speed up the arrival of your next course . . .

e) Sorry, can you say all that again . . . ?

f) Mrs Hyde's just popped out of the office. Perhaps you could ring later?

2 Write a brief guide to be used by employees operating a telephone information service in a local leisure centre.

6.11 Dealing with customer complaints

Develops knowledge and understanding of the following element:

6.4   Deliver and evaluate customer service in leisure and tourism organisations

Supports development of the following core skills:

Communication 3.1 (Task 1)

Communication 3.2 (Task 2)

'The customer is always right' is an expression still commonly heard in service and other industries. Although an individual shop assistant or booking clerk may not always feel sympathetic to this view, there are a number of reasons why companies are increasingly concerned that customer complaints are handled with tact and diplomacy.

Customers are essential for the survival of any business and dissatisfied customers tend to go elsewhere. If their complaints are resolved successfully, they are more likely to feel that their needs and rights have been respected. The companies may also benefit by increasing the number of customers who use them again and by improving the quality of the services they offer. Additionally the company may actually enhance its reputation as a result of demonstrating that it can respond quickly and sensitively to customers' difficulties. Individual employees can gain greater job satisfaction if they are able to satisfy customers that things they have complained about will be put right.

The attitude of staff towards individual complaints is sometimes based on the assumption that these have little overall impact. Many dissatisfied customers do not voice their particular grievances, perhaps wishing to avoid confrontation. They are unlikely to return! Others will vent their frustration by telling all their friends and acquaintances, all of whom may be actual or potential customers of the same organisation. It could be argued that such customers can easily be replaced but, once marketing costs are taken into account, it is more expensive to attract new customers than to retain existing ones. Clearly there are some complainants who are out to be difficult, but research suggests that the majority simply want a reasonable response to their complaints and an improved service for themselves and others. They may actually feel that their complaint is for the good of the company. Complaining does, after all, take time and effort and often involves cost.

People will complain about a whole variety of things. In leisure and tourism complaints could include:

- the lack of a promised view from a hotel balcony
- a delayed flight
- increased charges on badminton court hire
- poor quality restaurant food.

Many complaints concern people who are supposedly working for the good of their customers. Rudeness or indifference offends people, particularly when they are seeking advice or information. When customers who already have a genuine complaint are met with rudeness or indifference, it is likely to provoke confrontation. This is particularly harmful to a company's image if it happens in a public place.

The best immediate response to most complaints is an offer of help. Establishing some kind of rapport can be useful. Many companies suggest ways of developing a genuinely sympathetic manner. Most would say it is important to 'own the problem' and not attempt to pass the blame onto someone else. Certainly employees should explain who they are and then establish the details of the complaint. Writing these down both allows the employee to clarify the facts and also gives them time to think about their response. It also suggests that the employee is interested in the problem and wishes to know what the customer would like to see done about it.

If genuine help is to be given, employees need to be fully aware of company policy. It is no use offering a compensatory free holiday to a complainant if the company then refuses to pay for it. Staff who deal with complaints do need to show that they are capable of some positive remedial action, whether it is offering a refund, a future credit or a replacement product. False promises, blaming others or putting off customers in the hope that they will lose interest in complaining may bring temporary relief but will all probably lose the company business in the long run. Many companies now have quality systems which guarantee that they will respond to complaints within a set time. Individual departments may receive pay bonuses or other incentives for meeting these targets consistently.

Your tasks

1 Working with a partner, take alternate roles of complainant and employee in the following situations:
   - a returning holidaymaker complaining to a travel agent that the sandy beach, as described in the brochure from which the holiday was booked, was in fact shingle
   - the user of a sports hall badminton court complaining to the receptionist that it was impossible to play with a trampoline in use in an adjacent area
   - an airline passenger complaining to a member of the cabin staff about the noise made by a small child sitting with its parents in the row opposite.

   Discuss what you think would be the best approach for the company employee to take in each case.

2 Choose a specific leisure and tourism context and write a series of guidance notes to help employees in that context deal with angry customers.

Unit 7 Health, safety and security in leisure and tourism

7.1 Health and safety: Chessington World of Adventures

Develops knowledge and understanding of the following element:

7.1 Investigate health, safety and security in leisure and tourism

Supports development of the following core skills:

Communication 3.1, 3.2 (Task 1)

Communication 3.2 (Task 2)

Over a million visitors and a thousand employees visited or worked at Chessington World of Adventures in 1991. Given the presence of wild animals and of a range of mechanical rides, health and safety are critical factors in the management and development of the attraction.

Chessington Zoo started life in 1931 as a small private collection of animals. Pearsons plc bought the expanded collection in 1975 and the group expanded its interests in the leisure industry by buying Madame Tussauds in 1978. A multi-million pound investment transformed Chessington into a theme park, although the collection of animals was largely retained. The attraction opened for the first time as Chessington World of Adventures in 1987.

The mixed nature of the site means that there are five maintenance areas involved, all of which carry a health and safety responsibility:

- buildings maintenance
- gardens maintenance
- rides maintenance
- vehicle maintenance
- site cleaning.

It also means that plumbers, carpenters, labourers, engineers, electricians and cleaners are all employed, as well as the employees working directly with the public.

Chessington World of Adventures Limited has a number of responsibilities under the Health and Safety at Work Act (1974).

- Safe and healthy working conditions must be provided for employees, including training to enable them to carry out their duties safely and efficiently.
- Safety devices and protective equipment must be available and their use must be supervised.
- The company consults its own employees, either individually or through their representatives, to make sure that safe and healthy working practices continue to be used.

To carry out these responsibilities at Chessington, a Health and Safety Committee has been appointed. Its objectives are to turn the legislation into safe practice by developing safe operating systems, safe working places and safe usage and storage of equipment. For these things to be done effectively the objectives must be communicated through training, supervision and written instruction.

It is not, however, only the company itself which has legal responsibilities. The Act also applies to employees who are required to co-operate with company safety policies and recommendations. This may be by wearing appropriate protective clothing, reporting hazards, or helping in investigating accidents.

At Chessington the General Manager is answerable to the Board for the safety performance of the attraction. Day-to-day responsibilities are delegated to managers and supervisors. They must apply safety rules such as checking equipment, investigating accidents and inspecting repairs. They must also ensure that all staff are familiar with the specific instructions which apply in different areas of

The Vampire, the hanging rollercoaster at Chessington World of Adventures.

the site and in the event of any emergency. Specific instructions cover procedures in the case of fire or an animal escaping. Training in the operation of fire equipment and emergency procedures is undertaken by the Safety Officer and the appropriate departmental manager. There are strict rules about entering animal cages or enclosures and, except in the case of an emergency, animal keepers must give their consent for any other member of staff to enter. If an accident should happen, staff are trained to know from where first aid can be requested and who to contact if outside help is needed. An investigation will be held to find out the cause of the accident and how to avoid any repetition.

Materials and machinery can be hazardous and great care is taken at Chessington to ensure that both are safe. New machinery is thoroughly tested before it is used. If new materials are potentially hazardous, instruction sheets on the safest way to use them are prepared and circulated.

Ride safety is particularly important. A practice similar to the pre-flight checks operated by airlines is used to ensure that rides are always in safe working order. A form known as a DID (Daily Inspection Document) indicates the nature of any repair or maintenance work carried out and creates an accurate record of the performance of machinery. New rides are only bought from reputable constructors; Chessington's engineers will recommend specifications of their own if they think a particular design has any potential risk, however remote. Drivers of the rides undergo thorough training and must pass written and practical tests before they are allowed to operate the rides. This training also includes learning how to diagnose potential mechanical faults and also how to carry out safe evacuation procedures.

Employees' specific responsibilities include:

- vehicle drivers keeping within speed limits
- catering staff doing everything to ensure the highest standards of hygiene: any suggestions which they might have for improving safety are encouraged
- employees working with the animals have to be aware of the dangers of wounds, especially where the animals may be carriers of diseases like hepatitis B. They have to be particularly careful when animals are being treated, especially if they are being injected with powerful anaesthetics!

Environmental Health Officers are charged with administering the 1981 Zoo Licensing Act. In particular this involves checking that the standards maintained in the cages are acceptable.

As with many things dangerous to health, prevention is often better than cure. Chessington's safety policy emphasises good organisation and management:

- giving detailed attention to proper storage procedures
- inspecting machine safety devices regularly
- servicing animal cages regularly
- competent personnel regularly examining and testing electrical equipment and wiring.

Anything found to be defective has to be withdrawn from service until faults are put right, even if this means stopping a popular ride in the middle of a busy summer's day.

Your tasks

1 In what ways might the visiting public contribute to accidents at zoos or leisure parks with mechanical rides?

Suggest a number of ways of trying to reduce the possibility of accidents involving visitors.

What are the practical issues which attraction managers would have to confront before deciding whether each of your suggestions was worth investing in?

2 Specific safety instructions are to be issued to employees at a theme park like Chessington. Make some notes which could be used as a basis for these instructions for each of the following groups:
- gardeners
- site cleaners
- vehicle maintenance staff.

7.2 Health and safety: caves open to the public

Develops knowledge and understanding of the following element:
7.1 Investigate health, safety and security in leisure and tourism

Supports development of the following core skills:
Communication 3.2 (Task 1)
Communication 3.1 (Task 2)
Communication 3.2 (Task 3)
Communication 3.2 (Task 4)

When people are inside buildings, for business or leisure, many issues concerning health and safety will be similar. For example, the occupants will need as much protection as possible in the event of fire or accidents. Natural attractions like caves are not designed to be occupied by people. They present Health and Safety Officers, as well as the companies which manage the sites, with a number of distinctive challenges.

The shape of the cave itself may present some obvious hazards. The height of some parts of the roof may be below average head height and there may be sharp, jagged stones in both the roof and walls. Caves are often dimly lit, especially in the narrower passages, and clear guidance is essential if injuries are to be avoided. This means not only indicating where visitors should lower their heads but also pointing out accurately the distance they should step before standing upright again. The ground underfoot may also be uneven. Steps have often been cut into rock and the height of each step can differ. Caves have often been created as a result of river systems cutting through rock formations and pathways may therefore be damp and slippery. Guides will need to point out any particularly difficult spots, and, where possible, handrails will need to be fitted to make steps and slopes easier to negotiate.

Lighting is important: a party of visitors trying to find its way out of a series of caves in complete darkness would be at serious risk of injury. At Wookey Hole Caves, in Somerset, lighting is fixed a foot above floor level so that visitors can see where they are walking. Other lights are fixed into the walls of the caves in order to illuminate their most

The Great Hall, Wookey Hole Caves.

interesting features. Each guide carries a torch and there is a back-up lighting system which can operate independently for up to eight hours in the event of mains failure. There are telephones at regular intervals through the cave system so that guides can contact the surface should they need to do so.

Most underground cave systems, natural or the result of industrial mining, contain areas considered unsafe for the general public. These may be steep shafts, for example, or areas of deep water. Visitors are generally kept away from these by strong mesh fencing and sometimes spoken and written warnings as well.

Most cave systems open to the public generally have a natural safety advantage if they contain bottlenecks, which may be narrow passages, or single track bridges built across chasms or underground lakes and rivers. Visitors have to move slowly and carefully through these parts of the cave system.

One fairly new issue which the owners of caves open to the public have had to consider is the possible presence of radon gas. This radioactive material exists naturally underground and in some circumstances has been known to build up to concentration levels which need to be monitored. There are already regulations governing the levels of radon gas found in mines. These are quite strict, since dust acts as a carrier of the gas and its concentration may be higher than in caves where the type of rock formation makes its presence a possibility.

The Health and Safety Executive is currently discussing with the British Association of Show Caves how to set levels for caves. Readings are taken regularly and there is a system of grading them.

- At the first level the Health and Safety Executive has to be notified.
- At the second the public has to be made aware.
- At the third level access has to be restricted.

However, the actual risk to an individual visitor is thought to be extremely low; much less than, say, exposure to sunlight. Guides will of course spend much more time underground than individual visitors, but at Wookey Hole, for example, it is estimated that each guide spends 1000 hours underground and the safety level is set at 6000 hours. Guides will sometimes carry equipment to monitor radon levels, since these vary according to temperature and humidity. Good ventilation also keeps the air clear. The cave system open to the public leaves the hillside at a different point from the entrance, which means that the ventilation system draws air in at one end of the system and expels it at the other.

Nine chambers at Wookey Hole are now open to the public, but a further sixteen were discovered between 1948 and 1976. These are only accessible to divers with breathing equipment and all visits are controlled by the British Cave Diving Group. Visibility underwater is limited, particularly once the mud on the bottom has been disturbed. A bright orange rope runs through the chambers, some of which are very narrow, in order to help divers to find their way back. Divers who want to reach the last chamber have to attach breathing equipment to their thighs so that they can squeeze through the narrower gaps. At the end of the system there is an abyss which descends more than 200 feet. Such a descent would require a special breathing mixture and regular stops for decompression on the ascent.

Your tasks

1 Write the text of a notice to be displayed at the entrance to Wookey Hole Caves, intended to ensure the safety of visitors.

2 Identify the risks which you think visitors to each of the following five types of natural attraction might face:
- cliffs (for example Beachy Head, Land's End)
- beaches (for example Blackpool, Margate, Newquay)
- mountains (for example Snowdonia)
- moors (for example Exmoor, North Yorkshire Moors)
- lakes (for example Windermere, Loch Ness).

3 For each type of natural attraction, list the risks in rank order, beginning with what you think is the most dangerous and working down to the least serious.

4 Choose a specific natural attraction which falls into one of the five categories listed in Task 2. Write a report explaining the possible health and safety risks for visitors to your chosen site. You should include proposals of measures intended to reduce the level of those risks to a minimum.

7.3 Effects of European legislation on restaurant health and safety practice

Develops knowledge and understanding of the following element:
7.1 Investigate health, safety and security in leisure and tourism

Supports development of the following core skills:
Communication 3.2 (Task 1)
Communication 3.2 (Task 2)
Communication 3.1 (Task 3)
Communication 3.2 (Task 4)
Communication 3.2 (Task 5)

The food industry in the UK has been governed by laws and regulations for many years. Broadly speaking these are concerned with:
- the production or sale of food unfit for consumption
- the contamination of food
- the hygiene of food premises, equipment and personnel
- hygiene practices, including temperature control and treatment
- the control of food poisoning and food-borne diseases
- the composition and labelling of food.

The Food Safety Act 1990 makes it illegal to sell food which may injure health, or food which has been falsely described or labelled. Food operators accused of breaking this law may offer 'due diligence' as a defence if they can demonstrate that they have taken reasonable precautions. These precautions may include controls, efficient operating systems, records, training, testing and codes of practice.

Restaurants have been subject to a number of new sets of regulations in recent years. The Food Hygiene (General) Regulations 1990 are used to control standards of hygiene in food premises. These regulations cover cleanliness and condition of premises, the suitability of equipment and containers, the personal hygiene of all food handlers, washing facilities, water supply, sanitation and food exposure. Precise temperature controls for a range of perishable foods, for example dairy products, were included in the Food Hygiene (Amendment) Regulations 1990/1. The Food Premises (Registration) Regulations 1991 required food premises to register with their local authority.

Restaurants are subject to the same health and safety laws and regulations as other businesses. They must observe the Health and Safety at Work Act 1974, which requires them to ensure the health, safety and welfare of employees and customers. Supervision and training are required for all staff operating or cleaning dangerous machines, such as gravity feed slicers. The Control of Substances Hazardous to Health Regulations 1988 set out measures to protect employees and members of the public from hazardous substances. In catering establishments these might include gas cylinders or concentrated cleaning fluids.

It is in this area of health and safety that restaurants are now having to face new EU Directives which came into force in the UK in 1993. The Directives, which must become law in all the countries in the European Union, cover these seven areas:

- the management of health and safety at work
- health, safety and welfare in the workplace
- manual handling operations
- the use of display screen equipment at work
- fire precautions in places of work
- the provision and use of work equipment
- personal protective equipment at work.

The main terms of these Directives are as follows.

The management of health and safety at work regulations

These place a responsibility on employers to assess risks to employees and take measures to ensure their protection. These measures must include emergency procedures, reliable means of communicating health and safety information to employees, and suitable health and safety training.

Health, safety and welfare in the workplace

These govern the conditions of the working environment, including temperature, ventilation, lighting, room sizes and work stations. Areas where temperatures are naturally high, such as restaurant kitchens, must be subject to measures to reduce the level of discomfort to employees. All aspects of the work premises – including floors, gangways, windows, doors, partitions, stairs, escalators and fitments – must be safe. Appropriate facilities must be provided for employees. These have to include toilets, washing facilities, space for hanging clothing, seating and rest areas. All workplaces have to be properly maintained and cleaned.

Manual handling operations

Employees must not be required to lift unreasonably heavy loads manually. Where manual lifting is unavoidable the risks of injury should be kept to a minimum by proper assessment of the load, the lifting task, the space available and the number of people required to do the job safely.

The use of display screen equipment at work

These regulations are intended to protect the increasing number of employees who use a VDU screen for a substantial part of their working day. The working environment needs to be comfortable and the equipment used should not be of a low standard. Regular breaks should be available and frequent VDU users should also be provided with regular eye tests. The employer should pay for standard frames or lenses if the tests prove that these are required for VDU work.

Fire precautions in places of work

Restaurants represent a high risk in terms of fire and this Directive requires them to prepare an emergency plan. It should contain details of the means of fire fighting available, such as sprinklers. It also has to include instruction to employees in the event of a fire, evacuation procedures and arrangements for calling in the fire services. Fire escapes have to be kept clear of obstacles. Staff should receive training in the use of fire extinguishers and fire drills should take place at least once a year.

Provision and use of work equipment

Employers must ensure that suitable equipment is available and that it is only used for the purpose for which it was purchased. Equipment must be properly maintained, and staff using it must be given adequate information, instruction and training. Where dangerous machinery, such as a slicer, is in use proper guards and protective devices must be attached. Maintenance of equipment should not be carried out while it is in use. There should not be a risk to employees if the equipment should fail to operate at any point.

Your tasks

The final area covered by these Directives relates to personal protective equipment at work. Various types of protection are described, relating to different parts of the body which might be at risk from injury at work. These are summarised in the table on page 69.

1 List the main risks of physical injury which workers in a busy restaurant kitchen might face.

2 For each risk listed give an example of an item of protective clothing which would, in the event of an accident, reduce their chances of injury to the minimum.

3 Discuss how practical it would be for all employees in the kitchen to wear all the items of protective equipment you have listed at all times and under all working conditions.

4 List what you consider to be essential items of personal protective equipment to be worn by employees performing different tasks in the kitchen.

5 Write a short report outlining the guidance which should be offered about the nature, materials and quality of this equipment, and about when and how it should be worn.

Part of the body	Types of personal protective equipment	Examples of injury risks
head	crash helmets industrial safety helmets caps hairnets	road accident falling objects striking fixed obstacles entanglement in machinery
eyes	safety spectacles eyeshields safety goggles faceshields	impact splashes from hot liquids chemical mists and sprays dust
feet	safety boots clogs Wellington boots anti-static footwear	sharp objects on the floor dropping heavy objects slipping spilling hot liquids
hands	rubber gloves leather gloves cotton gloves thermal protection gloves	burns cuts and abrasions contact with toxic or corrosive liquids allergies and dermatitis
body	overalls aprons high visibility clothing thermal clothing	splashes from oils and fats effects of excessive heat or cold spillages cuts

7.4 The work of an EHO

Develops knowledge and understanding of the following element:
7.1 Investigate health, safety and security in leisure and tourism

Supports development of the following core skills:
Application of number 3.2; Communication 3.1 (Task 1)
Application of number 3.1; Communication 3.2; Information Technology 3.3 (Task 2)

The Health and Safety Executive is responsible for workplace safety in places like factories, farms, mines, fairgrounds, railways and building sites; local government Environmental Health Officers, however, currently cover health and safety issues in shops, offices, hotels, restaurants and leisure centres.

One of the many responsibilities of an Environmental Health Officer is the prevention of risk either in or near the workplace. The Health and Safety at Work Act (1974) and the regulations to enforce it mean that an EHO has to check that both those involved in commercial activities and those living nearby are not exposed to risk. This means checking that the following areas of the workplace reach the accepted standards:

- cleanliness
- temperature
- ventilation
- lighting
- washing and toilet facilities
- safety of machinery and materials.

If an employee is injured in a non-industrial workplace the EHO is responsible for investigating the accident. The employer is responsible for ensuring that machinery is not dangerous and that ventilation and lighting are sufficient for tasks to be performed safely. If the EHO decides that working conditions are not satisfactory, he or she can invoke the law to make sure that improvements are made.

Food service is a critical part of the leisure and tourism industries, and it is the Environmental Health Officer's job to ensure that food supplies are clean and safe. They have to check that all stages of food production, from slaughter or harvesting right through to public consumption, do not allow dangerous impurities to appear. Hotels, restaurants, public houses, food shops and mobile food outlets are inspected to see that they are not carrying contaminated food. An EHO will investigate complaints about bad food or dirty eating places and, if it is found necessary, take legal proceedings against the offenders. They will also attempt to trace the origin of any reported cases of food poisoning, suggesting how risks of any future outbreaks from the same source can be reduced.

Environmental Health Officers also monitor cases of air pollution and excessive noise. For example, people living near airports may suffer considerable disruption to their daily lives as a result of aircraft noise. The EHO will be able to advise them whether or not they qualify for a local authority grant to insulate their homes against the noise. He or she may also advise on planning applications for leisure developments, such as sports stadia or night clubs, where the local residents fear that noise will increase to the point where it threatens their normal daily lives.

Travel may also be responsible for small scale but serious health risks. Occasionally people who have been abroad return with infectious diseases. The EHO, having taken specialist medical advice, may need to ensure that the victim is kept in isolation so that other lives are not put at risk. The EHO will also carry out health checks at ports. The officer looks particularly at imported foodstuffs to see that they are free of vermin or other infestations. The EHO has legal power to rid premises of pests such as rats, mice and insects.

Environmental Health Officers have a number of smaller, specialist duties which particularly concern leisure and tourism:

- to check that water supplies and swimming pools are clean and wholesome
- to inspect and grant licences to centres where there are live animals, for example equestrian centres
- to check retail premises, including those catering specifically for tourists, to ensure that their products are safe and hygienic
- to check the standards at camping and caravan sites before issuing the licence the sites need to operate.

Some EHOs also have responsibilities for the standards of accommodation offered on canal and other leisure boats.

Your tasks

1 List the ways in which a new camping and/or caravan site might affect a rural
environment.

Discuss each possible effect under the following headings:

a) how serious you think it will be

b) the possible measures which could be taken to counter it

c) the likely cost and viability of each of the proposed measures.

2 The owner of an intended new camping and/or caravan site needs to assess whether
they have fully considered all the relevant health and safety issues. Draw up a
questionnaire which will help them to do this.

7.5 Health and safety, and the provision of in-flight catering

Develops knowledge and understanding of the following element:

7.1 Investigate health, safety and security in leisure and tourism

Supports development of the following core skills:

Application of number 3.2; Communication 3.1 (Task 1)
Communication 3.4 (Task 2)
Communication 3.2 (Task 3)
Communication 3.2, 3.3 (Task 4/5)

Airlines have traditionally supplied meals on all flights except very short ones. In some
cases the length of the flight would make this a necessity anyway. From the passengers'
point of view it may also help to relieve some of the monotony of spending a long time in
a confined space.

The kind of meal served on a flight will depend on the time of day and on the length of
the flight. Breakfast or lunch might be offered on a short flight, but a long-haul flight
would require several different meals to be served. The airline will have to decide the most
appropriate time to serve these, not an easy task where several time zones are crossed.

The main health and safety problems in providing in-flight catering arise from the need
to store, transport, heat and serve these meals. The process has to be carried out without
occupying too much space on the aircraft or adding too much weight to the load it has to
carry. Hygiene is of critical importance, particularly in view of the transportation of the
food and the huge number of meals individual catering operations have to produce each day.

The food is generally prepared and packaged in advance by a catering unit near to or at
an airport. They will give an exact specification to their suppliers. This will include very
precise demands about the weight, colour, freshness, quality and quantity of the produce to
be delivered to them. On delivery these supplies go immediately into a store which
includes an area maintained at a very low temperature to protect perishable goods. Food
products are very rarely stored for more than 24 hours.

Passengers being served a meal on board an aeroplane.

Hot meals are cooked in a kitchen and then rapidly chilled to a temperature of about 5 degrees centigrade within 90 minutes. Probes are used to test the temperatures and any items which have not cooled rapidly enough are thrown away. Meals are covered, usually in foil wrappings, and most will have been consumed within 24 hours of being cooked. Once on the aircraft meals are rapidly reheated to a temperature of 70 degrees centigrade within 30 minutes. Speed and correct temperature control are critical in preventing the development of harmful bacteria.

The preparation of in-flight catering is extremely labour intensive. This is largely because each food item has to be separately placed in the right place on a tray, plate or container by hand. A single Boeing 747 flight may carry as many as 25 000 catering items! Some idea of the scale of in-flight catering operations can be deduced from the fact that in a single day in 1993 Forte Airport Services at Heathrow used 1500lb of iceberg lettuce and the equivalent of 5000 eggs.

Staffing an in-flight catering service can present managers with a challenge. Some of the tasks involved in food preparation are very repetitive and the fact that airlines require the service to operate up to 18 hours a day means that shift work is inevitable. Punctilious observance of all health and safety regulations is also demanded of employees.

One of the advantages of locating an in-flight catering company on the perimeter of an airport is that the food spends less time being transported. The catering companies can react more easily to late changes in passenger lists. Though airlines notify the in-flight caterers of how many passengers are travelling on each flight, making sure that all the food arrives in the right place at the right time is a complicated business. Flight delays and cancellations can cause considerable problems. The food is transported on specially constructed lorries which have ramps inside, enabling their loads to be lifted to the level of the aircraft doors. The planes are considered too valuable to risk allowing drivers to reverse lorries towards them!

Most in-flight caterers use moulded plastic trays with different containers for separate parts of the meal and generally with a transparent plastic cover, thus saving on cleaning and washing-up costs. It also makes it safer for cabin crew to carry the food inside the aircraft, reducing the risk of spillages. Trays, sauces and condiments are all thrown away after use. The crockery, cutlery and glasses used in first and business class areas, and any metal cutlery used in other classes, along with the trolleys used to transport the meals along the aircraft, all go through an automated and very thorough washing process.

Once a flight is over all used equipment and uneaten food is cleared from the plane. The food is treated as unsuitable for any further use and is thrown away. A further precaution requires companies supplying airline food to agree to regular analysis of samples taken from the meals they provide. These will be sent to a food science laboratory where they will be checked for any kind of contamination.

In-flight caterers have to supply meals which meet a range of different health requirements, including meeting any demand for special diets. This includes meeting special requirements which may be either a matter of personal taste, as with vegetarians, or of religious belief, as with kosher meals. Individual passengers may request separate meals on medical grounds, for example fat-free or salt-free diets. Some airlines offer special children's meals, with smaller portions and ingredients which are thought to be popular with children.

Since passengers may feel that one flight is much the same as another, airlines are conscious that food and food service may be one means by which they distinguish one airline from its competitors. Menus are changed regularly and return flights will always offer a different choice from outbound ones. On some routes seasonal changes are reflected in menus with items like summer salads replacing winter hot meals.

Your tasks

A regional airline is planning a new scheduled service between East Midlands Airport (nearest cities Derby, Nottingham and Leicester) and Milan in Northern Italy.

An outward bound flight will leave for Italy at 9 a.m. and the return flight will depart from Milan at 5 p.m.

1 Calculate the approximate time that passengers will spend in the air and then assess what proportion of this could realistically be spent in serving meals.

2 Decide the type of meals which would be appropriate for economy class and business class passengers on the outward, and on the return flights.

3 List six examples of specific dishes you think would be inappropriate to offer on this service, because of the potential health and safety risks they might carry.

4 Choose either business or economy class and then draw up two sample menus, one for a meal suitable for the outward flight and one suitable for the return.

List the ingredients needed and the quantities required for each portion.

5 Write an outline of the content and text for a training video, to be used with new employees by the in-flight caterer providing meals on this airline service.

The video should address general health and hygiene issues in relation to food preparation, and provide guidance on the preparation and storage of specific dishes.

7.6 Activity holidays: customer safety

Develops knowledge and understanding of the following element:
7.2   Ensure the health and safety of a leisure and tourism event

Supports development of the following core skills:
Communication 3.2 (Task 1)
Application of number 3.2; Communication 3.2 (Task 2)
Communication 3.2 (Task 3)

The days when people spent their whole holiday asleep in a deck chair are, for many, long gone. Travel brochures now advertise tours in which people can try white water canoeing, hot air ballooning, abseiling or even driving racing cars. Tour operators who offer these activities can do a number of things to make them as safe as possible, apart from investing in very sound insurance schemes.

● The qualifications and skills of the staff they hire are vital: a non-swimming water ski instructor, for example, would be a severe liability.
● The activity centres should be required to record all accidents and provide a full explanation of how and why each one occurred.
● Supervision needs to be thorough: centres need to allow for the fact that many accidents happen at times when no formal activity or instruction is taking place, particularly where children are involved.

Two types of activity holiday which carry particular risk of injury are pony-trekking and water sports. Ponies may look sweet, biddable creatures in travel brochures, but they can be obstinate and unpredictable. Since trekking is often across rough and remote terrain, the consequences of being thrown can be very serious. The hot summers of 1990 and 1991 led to an increase of algae in many stretches of fresh water. Anyone taking part in water sports who swallowed any of this could suffer serious after-effects. In spite of this there is no legal requirement for staff at activity centres to have first aid qualifications.

The Department for Education has published a document called Safety in Outdoor Pursuits which recommends safety procedures for outdoor holiday centres. It covers points and suggestions such as the following:

● the most appropriate ratios of leaders or instructors to students on different activities
● careful inspection of the training and qualifications claimed by instructors
● high standard and regular inspection of equipment.

Activities like skiing carry higher risks of injury than many others, not all of them due to slippery conditions under foot. The most common injuries suffered are pulled muscles and twisted joints, but there could be fewer of these if holiday-makers followed training programmes aimed at improving their fitness before they set off. Skiing falls can be caused by incompetence, but are often due to fatigue as well. Exercises like running or cycling can improve individual stamina and reduce the risk of falls resulting from tiredness.

Your tasks

Mr Wally Tempty owns a remote hill farm in North Wales. In recent years he has found it increasingly difficult to make a decent living from farming. He applied for and gained planning permission to renovate a barn on his land and convert it to dormitory-style accommodation for 20 visitors.

The farm is 30 miles from the village of Llanmad, where shops and the local doctor can be found. The regional hospital and fire services are a further 20 miles away in Abersynglais. He proposed to lay out a dirt race track over hilly ground (see the sketch map below). His proposal was accepted largely because his farm is so remote. He has now completed the track and has bought six mountain bikes and six motor cycle scramblers, all second hand.

He has marketed his facilities largely to appeal to youth club and school parties.

1 List the potential hazards involved in Mr Tempty's scheme to encourage people to come and stay on his farm.

2 Draw up a series of proposals which you think would reduce the risks as far as possible. Comment on their cost and how practical they would be.

3 Write a contingency plan for Mr Tempty and any staff he employs to follow in the event of an accident or emergency.

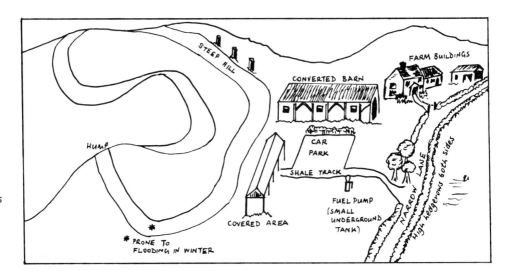

Mr Wally Tempty's sketch map of his farm, showing his development proposals.

7.7 Fireworks at Alton Towers

Develops knowledge and understanding of the following element:
7.2 Ensure the health and safety of a leisure and tourism event

Supports development of the following core skills:
Communication 3.1, 3.4 (Task 1)
Communication 3.2, 3.3 (Task 2)

Among the many special events hosted by Alton Towers is a firework display. This requires thorough planning both because of the large numbers attending and also because of the nature of the event itself.

The first planning meeting for the event starts with a debrief of the previous year's event. A capacity is set and the latest regulations on Safe Practice for the Management of Outdoor Events, produced by the Health and Safety Executive, are carefully checked.

At this stage it is also important to establish the likely profitability of the event. Overheads are calculated, including stewarding and security costs, cleaning, extra lighting and signage for the event, mobile catering units, products and staffing for any merchandising activities, and additional radios to meet extra communication needs. Items such as cleaning will be particularly expensive since the Leisure Park will have to be open to the public the next day and cleaning teams will have to operate very late at night and then at first light the next day.

The fireworks display takes the form of a show with a series of scenes which first have to be designed. Once the content and length is agreed, accompanying music is chosen and timed. At this point three outside companies are contracted. A pyrotechnical company plans and makes the fireworks, a lighting and laser company plans the visual effects and a third company plans the sound and public address systems. Eight weeks before the event a technical meeting is called in which all the elements of the show are drawn together. A technical rehearsal is held two days before the event to check the sound and lighting. One track on the eight-track recording system used is

Fireworks display at Alton Towers.

reserved as a cue track, which enables all lighting and laser effects to be cued automatically.

A budget is set for the display, taking account of the experience of previous years and of the number of nights on which the display is to take place. Some of the costs have to be estimated. The fireworks themselves tend to be a fixed cost but the lighting costs will depend on the amount of time they are actually being used.

A firework display of this size would normally require an Entertainments Licence, which is not granted automatically. The terms of such a licence have to be negotiated and stipulations are laid down about crowd size, noise, access and toilet facilities. The licensing authority, in this case Staffordshire, would need to be satisfied about a range of health and safety issues. These would include a check on physical structures, such as staging and barriers, and electrical and mechanical installations. The sound emitted by the PA system has to be measured at various points around the site. Assurances about the safety of food and drink supplies would be sought, including a restriction on any materials thought to be potentially dangerous, such as bottles. Alton Towers, given the expanse of water on the site, is also required to have a lifeboat and lifeguards available.

Once the planning is under way contracts are drawn up between Alton Towers and other participating companies. As well as stipulating fees, these contracts lay down conditions about the use of the site. They cover insurance issues in the event of cancellation, injury, loss or damage. They insist on compliance with regulations, including the protection of grass areas by the use of trackway covers.

As the event draws near final schedules are drawn up. These include a fit-up schedule which gives accurate timings for the delivery and installation of equipment. An event schedule, circulated to all participating employees, gives detailed timings of all activities during the event itself. In the interests of maintaining good public relations, a letter is sent out just before the event to all the residents of the local villages, giving them notice of the event and offering them free tickets.

Your tasks

Lazydaze Leisure Park, situated about 20 miles from the nearest town and without a regular public transport service, nevertheless attracts visitors well into the autumn. Most of them are attracted by the permanent fairground, the sizeable boating lake and an attractive natural arena, flanked on two sides by grandstands and frequently used for open air displays and concerts.

The managers of the Park decide to hold an early evening firework display at a weekend towards the end of the season. In order to secure good attendance, a special offer ticket is made widely available, combining a reduced rate entrance to the fairground with a ticket for the firework display. This is expected to increase the number of daytime visitors, particularly in the afternoon.

I Study the map on page 78 and then discuss ideas for coping with the following issues and concerns which have been raised:

a) Equipment and materials will need to be brought in, and lighting and electrical work carried out, during the time when the Park is open to the public.

b) Some visitors will be inside the Park during the day with combined tickets; others

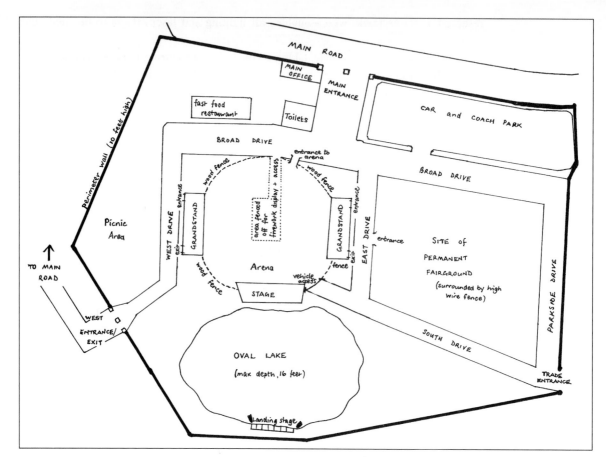

MAIN ROAD

MAIN
OFFICE

MAIN
ENTRANCE

CAR and COACH PARK

fast food
restaurant

Toilets

BROAD DRIVE

BROAD DRIVE

Perimeter wall (10 feet high)

entrance to
arena

wood fence

wood fence

entrance to
arena

WEST DRIVE

entrance

GRANDSTAND

exit

area fenced
off for
firework display + access

entrance

GRANDSTAND

exit

EAST DRIVE

entrance

SITE of

PERMANENT

Picnic
Area

wood fence

Arena

fence

FAIRGROUND

(surrounded by high
wire fence)

PARKSIDE DRIVE

TO MAIN
ROAD

wood fence

STAGE

vehicle
access

WEST
ENTRANCE/
EXIT

SOUTH DRIVE

OVAL LAKE

(max depth 16 feet)

TRADE
ENTRANCE

Landing stage

*Sketch map of
Lazydaze Leisure
Park.*

will arrive during the late afternoon wanting tickets for the firework display only.
The latter will have to be admitted to the Park as they can not be kept queuing on
the main road.

c) The car and coach park is unlikely to be able to accommodate all visitors if the
numbers predicted actually turn up.

d) Crowds could build up causing dangerous congestion in two places: in East
Drive where the entrance to the fairground faces the entrance to the grandstand
and on Broad Drive between the entrance to the arena and the toilets and
restaurant.

e) There is no segregation of cars and pedestrians in the area around the main
entrance.

f) The Security Department has expressed concern about the adequacy of the
fencing round the arena, though recognises that complete replacement may not
be affordable in the short term. They are also concerned about the difficulty of
patrolling the perimeter fence when staff will be needed elsewhere.

g) The siting of two additional mobile food outlets and a mobile toilet unit has still to
be agreed.

h) The footpaths around Oval Lake are easily accessible from both West and South
Drive, as is the landing stage where the small boats are moored.

2 Propose a suitable plan, with explanations, for each of the following event needs:

a) a safe and rapid evacuation procedure

b) a suitable site for a small medical unit, able to respond quickly to emergencies when the Park is at its most crowded

c) a plan to enable the fire service to respond quickly in an emergency, taking note of the evacuation procedure described in (a).

7.8 Security training for staff: Thorpe Park

Develops knowledge and understanding of the following element:
7.3 Ensure the security of a leisure and tourism event

Supports development of the following core skills:
Communication 3.2 (Task 1)
Communication 3.2, 3.3 (Task 2)
Communication 3.2 (Task 3)

Thorpe Park, a leisure park near Chertsey, in Surrey, receives more than a million visits a year. The site covers 500 acres, including large stretches of water, and visitors stay on average for six hours. All new employees undergo a training programme which stresses the importance of security. Staff are described as members of a cast, putting on a daily show for the benefit of the public. The extract below from Thorpe Park's training booklet *On with the Show* describes each employee's security responsibilities.

We are all responsible for maintaining the high level of security at Thorpe Park. Immediately report any thefts, loss of or damage to the Park's property to your Supervisor and Operations Control.

Be alert to suspicious incidents or people and report them at once.

If you find or are handed any lost property, immediately check for items of value in the presence of another person. All lost property must be handed in to the Visitor Services Point at the earliest opportunity and entered in the Lost Property Register. You are personally responsible for such property until it is handed in; therefore you should not leave it in your workplace overnight or hand it to another Cast Member. If you are unable to hand in an item of lost property immediately, particularly a valuable item such as a purse or handbag, telephone the Visitor Services Point to advise them that this item has been found.

Always be aware of the security of your own property.

Cast Members are not permitted to carry any money into the Park.

Female Cast Members may take a small make-up bag to work. Apart from this, Cast Members are not permitted to carry personal bags into the Park.

Random spot searches will be carried out.

Your security pass

Your security pass is an essential part of your costume. It enables you to:

- sign in and out for work
- obtain your costume
- obtain locker keys
- collect your till float (where applicable)
- cash a cheque at the Cast Control.

Your tasks

1 Devise an exercise, to be used as part of the training programme for new staff at a leisure park, to make them more aware of how to identify 'suspicious incidents or people'.

2 Outline a scheme to make visitors to a popular tourist attraction more conscious of protecting their own property against theft; remember that you do not want to give the impression that the attraction is completely unsafe to visit because of the high crime risk.

3 Some leisure and tourism facilities insist that staff wear visible identification, carrying their names, and sometimes photographs.

Choose several leisure and tourism workplaces and list the possible advantages and disadvantages of such a practice in each of them.

7.9 Preventing business crime

Develops knowledge and understanding of the following element:
7.3 Ensure the security of a leisure and tourism event

Supports development of the following core skills:
Communication 3.2 (Task 1)
Communication 3.2 (Task 2)
Communication 3.2 (Task 3)
Communication 3.2, 3.4 (Task 4)

Business crime prevention can be divided into three broad categories:
- physical methods
- community action
- design factors.

Physical methods include all the machinery and technology which can be used to make crime more difficult, such as alarms or surveillance systems. Community awareness can both reduce the risk of crime and increase the rate of conviction. Design, especially of buildings, can be used to persuade potential criminals that committing an offence in a particular environment is simply too risky.

About 95% of crime is committed against property rather than against the person. Most violent crimes occur after 11 o'clock at night when alcohol is often a factor. This means that, for managers of leisure and tourism companies, theft and fraud are the offences they will most likely have to deal with. Hotels and leisure centres must do all they can to make breaking into rooms or lockers and theft of luggage or handbags difficult.

Many tourism operations, for example attractions, are cash businesses. They face the same risk of robberies as banks, building societies and shops. They can make use of some of the technology developed to make robbery more difficult. Areas where counter staff work with the public, such as a currency exchange centre, can have rapid rising screens fitted. In less than a second these will place an opaque barrier between the would-be robber and the counter staff. Time lapse safes also have the effect of delaying the robber, few of whom will want to take the chance of waiting around for an hour or two until the safe can be opened again! These can be set for a shorter time lapse, so that customers genuinely wishing to withdraw or exchange cash can be asked to return in 10 or 15 minutes. Premises wishing to create a friendly, informal atmosphere may be reluctant to put up too many barriers between customers and staff. They can, however, still use electronic devices such as metal detectors installed in the entrance. These will indicate if anyone is carrying any larger than usual metal objects.

The physical movement of money from business premises to security vans represents a vulnerable point in protecting the cash. There are two technological developments which help in detecting this type of crime:

- a smoke and dye system will release smoke from cash bags, leaving a dye on the money and those handling it
- security vehicles can be fitted with surveillance systems which enable a monitor at a base station to pick up a signal from the vehicle. This means that its movements can be tracked accurately and any departure from the agreed route immediately passed on to the police.

Other technological advances have been employed in the fight against crime. In 1990 some £2 billion was spent by industry as a whole on security equipment. This included closed circuit television surveillance, electronic access control systems, electronic article surveillance (more commonly known as **tagging**), and alarm systems.

The access control systems are often used in hotels: swipe cards can be used to give limited or full access to hotel rooms to different staff, depending on whether their particular responsibilities require them to use specific rooms or areas.

Tagging can make the theft of valuable retail items more difficult by triggering an alarm if the goods are taken out of the shop. Some premises in the leisure industry house priceless items, like famous works of art. These can be protected by a curtain of invisible infrared beams which, if penetrated, will set off an alarm.

More sophisticated electronic equipment may be inappropriate, and too costly, for the many smaller operations which are part of the leisure and tourism industry. A small guest house, for example, will probably have to rely on more basic security. They will need to ensure that room keys are not left hanging in public places while guests are out. Locks should conform to British Standard 3621 which would lessen the chances of them being opened by a random selection of keys. Ground floor windows can be given some protection by planting dense, prickly shrubs beneath them, though these may make cleaning more difficult! Where the premises have a car park, the owners should try to ensure that cars are as visible as possible. They are also advised to put up signs advising visitors both to lock their cars and to remove any valuables from them.

Co-operation within local business communities can be valuable. Business watch schemes encourage property-marking so that the origin of stolen goods can be traced. Action against suspected theft is often not possible simply because property cannot be accurately identified. Reporting suspicious circumstances can reveal local criminal patterns and help to combat them. Conducting a regular **crime audit** can help to establish whether resources and materials are going missing, and more importantly, from where.

Some leisure and tourism companies also face a threat from terrorism. This may be a long-term threat based on the geographical location of the building or the nature of the business itself. Premises next to military offices carry a higher risk than average. The offices of some national airlines or shops selling animal furs may also be possible targets. The fact that Madame Tussauds and the Tower at Canary Wharf have been targeted by terrorist organisations emphasises that publicity is the terrorists' aim and any company with a high public profile should be aware of the threat. Sometimes the terrorist threat may be short-term. This might be the consequence of a visit from a well known public figure or from someone with military or diplomatic connections.

Measures to counter the threat of terrorism are often a matter of common sense. The basic security of buildings needs to be thorough. Problems often occur where several companies share premises and access is not controlled. There is often no reception area and the credentials of visitors are not checked, nor are they fetched and accompanied to the office of the person they have come to see. Premises like large office blocks and hotels need a **contingency plan**, known by all occupants, so that if they need to evacuate the building they can move rapidly to a safe place.

Some simple matters of good organisation can make terrorism more difficult:
- the more tidy a working area is, the more difficult it is to conceal explosive or fire-raising devices in it
- staff should always be alert
- staff should be sure to make eye-to-eye contact with customers: potential terrorists will feel less confident that they have remained unnoticed
- personnel taking incoming telephone calls need to be trained to handle bomb threats so that they extract as much information as possible. An easy way of doing this is to use a **pro forma** which suggests the questions they should ask and what they should listen out for. Accurate information about the location and timing of the threatened bomb is needed so that the company can make a quick response. The police would obviously hope for additional information about such things as accent, background noise, and what organisation the terrorist claimed to represent.

One of the main problems in dealing with business crime, particularly fraud, is the reluctance to report it. Few managing directors would wish to admit to shareholders that their companies had been defrauded. Leisure attractions face a different problem in admitting the threat of crime. People out for a pleasurable day do not want to be constantly reminded of the threat of pickpockets or car thieves.

The three principles of physical methods, community awareness and design are likely to guide the future of crime prevention.
- New physical means will be found, such as the plan to develop an air tube system which could move small sums of money from businesses direct to banks and which could be immediately shut down if they were tampered with.

- Building good community relations will continue to be a means of exchanging ideas on ways to prevent crime and raising the levels of awareness.
- Designers will work with architects to make sure that security features are built into new business premises.

Your tasks

1 Outline a proposal for an indoor event with a leisure and tourism focus, to take place in premises to which you have access. Make a careful tour of the premises, noting the locations which will be used, the access routes required, and the likely location of personnel and equipment needed.

2 List the potential security hazards you think running this event will involve.

3 Propose a series of measures to reduce risks and draw up a set of contingency plans to use in the event of emergencies.

4 Assess the potential viability of applying ideas and equipment mentioned in the extract about business crime in order to improve the security of your planned event.

7.10 Preventing theft in the hospitality industry

Develops knowledge and understanding of the following element:
7.3 Ensure the security of a leisure and tourism event

Supports development of the following core skills:
Communication 3.1, 3.4 (Task 1)
Communication 3.2, 3.3; Information Technology 3.1 (Task 2)

Some recent research suggested that as many as a quarter of the staff working in the hospitality industry are likely at some time to overcharge or cheat customers. The opportunities clearly exist, especially for employees operating in busy areas where surveillance is difficult. It is difficult to judge the extent of the problem since many such crimes go unreported. Prosecution might be a lesson to others, but hotel and bar owners often simply do not want the bad publicity it attracts.

The most common reasons given for staff theft are
- lack of regular supervision
- rapid turnover of cash
- the relatively low wages paid in many areas of hospitality.

Preventing such thefts can be approached in a number of ways.
- The **ethos** of the company and the effectiveness of the personnel department may significantly reduce or eliminate theft, especially in smaller operations.
- Using computerised tills will help, if the reports which they produce are studied carefully. If, however, employees intending to steal run reports to check that the exact amount has been removed from the till to cover the difference between what customers

83

paid and what the till registered, they may avoid discovery. Ironically, a busy till used by honest staff for a day will almost certainly show up small discrepancies.

- Observation of staff at work is the obvious way of preventing theft. Concealed video cameras can be used, though any method of surveillance is unlikely to uncover useful evidence if the staff under suspicion are aware that they are being watched.
- Another method is to set up customers to offer the exact money for an order. If they need change, employees have to open the till, but being handed the right money gives them an opportunity either to steal or to show their honesty.
- Searching the bags, pockets and lockers of employees is carried out by some companies, though to keep good staff relations companies who do this generally make this intention clear when any new member of staff is appointed.

If an employer reports a theft to the police, they will prosecute only if they believe that there is enough evidence to have a reasonable chance of securing a conviction. Some employers think that video surveillance and a policy of prosecuting all employees found guilty of theft is the best deterrent against future stealing. Others believe that the best ways to eliminate theft are to vet potential employees carefully, looking closely at references and past employment histories, and to provide training which emphasises the importance of personal integrity.

Your tasks

1 Look carefully at the following situations. Discuss what possible courses of action an event organiser might take and decide, in each case, which action you think would be the most appropriate:
- a cloakroom attendant at a county show fails to issue tickets for all garments received and, when challenged, claims that some coats were easily recognisable and therefore their owners didn't want to be bothered with tickets
- electronic tills are installed at the entrances to a major firework display – one till operator frequently uses the 'No sale' key and, when asked why, says that it is a way of using the till as an adding machine for working out larger orders
- an individual collecting money for a lottery intended to fund a centenary dinner for a sports club claims to have lost some unsold lottery tickets
- a car park attendant at an equestrian three-day event is reported by a member of the public for offering to resell three-day parking tickets on the second day of the event at a rate lower than the normal single day's parking fee – when asked for an explanation the attendant claims that the offer had come from the motorist who had seen him pick up the abandoned ticket.

2 Prepare a short talk to be given to part-time employees, taken on for the specific duration of an event, in which the following issues are covered:
- the rules and regulations which apply to this kind of event;
- the potential security hazards posed by the event;
- the standards expected of employees by the event organisers;
- the ways in which the organisers will monitor these standards.

Unit 8   Event management

8.1   Planning a festival: Commonwealth Day

Develops knowledge and understanding of the following element:
8.1   Propose options and select a feasible event

Supports development of the following core skills:
Communication 3.2, 3.4; Information Technology 3.3 (Task 1)
Communication 3.2, 3.4; Information Technology 3.3 (Task 2)
Communication 3.2 (Task 3)

Each year, during the early part of March, the Commonwealth Institute in London holds a Commonwealth Day. This event, first proposed by the Canadian Prime Minister Pierre Trudeau, is held in Commonwealth countries worldwide on the same day. The way in which it is organised reflects the main objective of the event: to celebrate the many different cultures of the 50 countries belonging to the Commonwealth. Children are encouraged to experience some of the sights, sounds and traditions of other countries. The festival builds on the underlying principle that greater international understanding is essential if world problems such as famine, disease, environmental damage and wars are ever to be eliminated.

The content of the Commonwealth Day Programme has to address two needs: how to make the Commonwealth better known to children and how to give each year's activities an interesting and topical focus. The first issue is partly met by the permanent exhibitions from all the Commonwealth countries on show within the Institute. These are supplemented on the day itself by the presence of representatives of those countries, usually members of the staff of their High Commissions. The second need is met by choosing a theme for each year's festival. Past Commonwealth Days have focused on such themes as sport, women in the Commonwealth, the Commonwealth view of Columbus and on new members of the Commonwealth such as Pakistan and Namibia. The use of a different theme each year adds variety but is also important for another reason. Children may find the principle of a Commonwealth too broad to grasp; concentrating on a particular theme may make this easier to understand.

Planning an event of this size requires agreement both about individual responsibilities and about the timetable for completing each stage of the preparations. Once the theme has been agreed, letters have to be sent to all High Commissioners requesting their co-operation. Some may need to be persuaded. The best ways of encouraging their participation or that of their staff is to stress the past success of the event and to offer guidance about what they might actually do. They can be encouraged to wear national dress, to teach children some words of their language and to distribute some information. Bringing too much to hand out to children may prove unhelpful in that it creates congestion in some areas of the exhibition hall. One way of avoiding congestion is to assign groups of students specific countries whose displays they must visit first.

If the event is to run smoothly, children need to be prepared for it as well as other participants. Those who intend to visit are sent advance notes explaining what the Commonwealth is and providing some background about the current year's theme. Guidance is offered about courtesy towards Commonwealth representatives, some of whom may be senior diplomats. The notes also contain some questions which children might like to ask about individual countries or about the festival theme. Teachers need information about the charge for attendance and advice about the best ways of getting to the Institute.

The Commonwealth Institute premises are open to the public all year round and so particular care has to be taken to ensure that the building itself can accommodate the event successfully. Parts of the building can be privately hired, so one of the first tasks in organising Commonwealth Day is to book all the required spaces – for example galleries, the lecture theatre and the lawn – well in advance. It is also important to know the number of staff who will be available to help on the day, in case extra part-time workers have to be hired. Fire regulations have to be checked to make sure that acceptable safety limits are set in terms of the numbers of visitors admitted overall and to individual areas like the film theatre.

A quantity of tickets and forms will have to be designed, made and distributed. When decisions are made about furniture layout, car parking arrangements, audio-visual aids, and artefacts to be delivered and exhibited, information about the arrangements agreed has to be sent to all personnel who will be affected. In the case of valuable artefacts, particularly where they are going to be handled by children, it may be necessary to arrange special insurance cover. Signs also have to be made and decisions taken about where these should be positioned. They need to be of good quality so that they both create a favourable impression of the occasion and also convey directional information clearly.

Generally the festival involves a number of events and performances. These need to be appropriate to the theme and, in the case of performances, they need to be monitored to ensure the quality and reliability of the performers. Events, such as the release of helium-

Commonwealth Day at The Commonwealth Institute.

filled balloons bearing the names of all the Commonwealth countries, need to have the right resources in the right place at the right time if they are to run smoothly.

Parallel to all this preparation is the marketing effort: Commonwealth Day will not be perceived as a great success if very few children turn up! The Institute has a Press Officer who will contact the media. Having a themed event is an advantage here in that journalists have a more obvious focus for a story. When a reassessment of Columbus was the theme in 1992, television news featured a school rap group taking part in the Commonwealth Day performance. Information about the festival is mailed to all schools.

Your tasks

Below is a draft timetable for Commonwealth Day Festival 1993.

Commonwealth Day Festival 1993   March 8th 1993

9.30	High Commission representatives arrive, set up displays and/or tables and have coffee with staff
10.00	Visit the Commonwealth – school groups have the chance to visit every country in the Commonwealth while remaining under one roof . . . . . . and to visit displays of work on this year's theme of *Human Values* brought by participating schools
11.45	Official opening by guest Commonwealth speaker, followed by dance/drama performances
12.30	Selected visitors proceed to lawn for balloon release
12.40	Balloon release
12.55	Director General's reception for High Commission representatives and other invited guests

Note: The theme for 1993 is Human Values and may touch on some or all of the following:
- legal, political and individual rights and whether these are equitably distributed
- the equal distribution of social and economic rights
- ecological and environmental rights, especially of future generations.

1 Write the text of a letter to be sent to all High Commissioners inviting them to participate in the 1993 Commonwealth Day Festival.

2 Write the text of a letter to be sent to all schools inviting them to apply to attend the 1993 Festival.

3 Propose an event or function to take place in your own locality to celebrate Commonwealth Day.

8.2 Organising a national festival

Develops knowledge and understanding of the following element:
8.1 Propose options and select a feasible event

Supports development of the following core skills:
Communication 3.1, 3.2 (Task 1)
Communication 3.2 (Task 2)
Communication 3.2, 3.3; Information Technology 3.1, 3.2, 3.3 (Task 3)

One of the first tasks given to the new government Department of National Heritage, when it was set up in early 1992, was to organise a European arts festival in Britain.

It was planned in the three-month period preceding its six month lifespan, from July to September 1992. A government grant of £6 million enabled some 1000 events to be staged at 250 different venues. Events included operatic performances, an arts trail, international theatre productions and a laser sculpture exhibition. The geographical spread of the events covered the whole of the United Kingdom.

The short time available for planning such a complex event meant that a number of organisations were approached for support. Regional Tourist Boards, the Arts Council and local authorities all suggested projects which might make appropriate contributions to the festival as a whole. These included new projects, as well as some which were already in existence but which could be enhanced by additional funding. Some event organisers wished to bring them under the wing of the festival, regardless of whether financial support was likely to be forthcoming.

The festival's main objective was to celebrate the United Kingdom's contribution to Europe's cultural heritage. Underlying that, however, was a desire to attract more people to develop an interest in the arts. The planners believed that young people especially received too little exposure to the arts and that much potential interest was therefore lost.

Two specific ways of meeting these broad objectives were tried. Educational and entertainment programmes in a variety of media formed the basis of a travelling exhibition which visited a number of less accessible locations around the UK. Publicity about the festival was mailed to 35 000 schools and 250 of the festival's events were intended to appeal specifically to young people.

The main problem faced by the festival organisers was the matter of publicising it effectively. It is much easier to advertise a one-week annual musical festival in a single town than it is to make people aware of a six-month programme spread around the whole country. An example of the problem is that public libraries have been used to distribute publicity material. However this means events are more likely to attract existing arts enthusiasts. They are less likely to come to the attention of the potential new audience which the festival planners originally had in mind.

Your tasks

1 Discuss which areas of the United Kingdom might have limited direct access to the arts.

a) Allocate a specific location to each student.

b) Identify a specific social issue to which a national organisation might wish to give wider publicity.

c) Assume that it has been decided that the best means of making an impact in the locations allocated is by drawing attention to the issue through all or some of the following:
- painting and sculpture
- dance
- drama
- literature
- music
- film.

Funds totalling £50 000 have been allocated to this particular venture.

Write a list of objectives for an arts event intended to have just such an impact.

2 Suggest three different schemes which would meet the objectives listed in Task 1. Each suggestion should explain the following:
- the format of the event
- how people would be encouraged to atttend
- what resources would be needed
- what the likely costs would be.

3 Prepare a short presentation outlining each of the three schemes and explaining, with reasons, which one would be most likely to achieve the main objectives proposed.

8.3 Government funding for sport in the community

Develops knowledge and understanding of the following element:

8.1   Propose options and select a feasible event

Supports development of the following core skills:

Application of number 3.1 (Task 1)

Communication 3.2 (Task 2)

Application of number 3.2; Communication 3.2, 3.3; Information Technology 3.1, 3.2, 3.3 (Task 3)

Communication 3.1 (Task 4)

In 1972 a Royal Charter established the Sports Council as an independent body whose main objectives were to increase participation in sport, to raise standards of performance, and to improve the quality and quantity of sports facilities. The Council is supported by a grant from the Government, although it also raises money from other sources.

    The Council is heavily involved in supporting coaching events in a wide range of sports. As part of its drive to make more facilities available to the community it has

Government sponsorship aims to encourage less traditional sports.

encouraged the opening up of more school facilities to the public, providing lighting and introducing artificial surfaces. It also produces research into the long-term demand for facilities and the effect of outreach work on socially disadvantaged groups.

In 1992 the Government announced further financial support to encourage the spread of sport in the community. £3 million has been contributed towards a sponsorship scheme called Sportsmatch. This scheme deliberately ignores national events and focuses on those planned for young people, especially those who might already be facing some sort of social disadvantage.

Planned sporting events which meet the criteria, and which do not already have an existing sponsorship arrangement, can apply for grants of up to £75 000, provided that they can find businesses which are willing to match the sum they are seeking. The intention of the scheme is to encourage financial support for sports other than the traditional ones which already appeal to spectators and hence are attractive to sponsors. One advantage of the scheme is that the support from businesses does not have to be cash. Their contribution can be through the provision of equipment, support services or rent-free premises.

Money for community sport also comes from local government, though their responsibility is largely the provision of facilities rather than of events. They may be willing to give financial support to national sporting events if they believe these will bring prestige or income to the region.

The issue which is often forgotten in debates about the funding of sport is the fact that the Government actually derives a significant income from it. Recent figures suggested it received £3.56 billion from a combination of sporting sources including VAT, income tax and National Insurance, excise and betting duty and corporation tax. This figure is claimed to be nearly seven times the amount spent by the Government on sport. Given the recorded growth of active participation in sport, many argue that government investment in it should be greater.

Your tasks

1 Conduct local research to establish which three sports, for which local facilities are not currently available, would be most attractive to the local community.

2 Plan a demonstration and/or coaching event intended both to give the community a chance to learn more about these sports and also to assess whether there is local talent or potential which deserves to be developed.

3 Make a presentation outlining each of your three proposals and addressing the following issues:
  - objectives
  - staffing
  - sources of funding
  - costs and income generated by the event itself
  - safety
  - publicity
  - potential take-up and capacity
  - follow up.

4 Appoint a different panel, made up of three students, for each presentation. Their task is to select the best of the three options and to justify their choice.

8.4 Planning event catering

Develops knowledge and understanding of the following element:
8.2 Plan an event as a team

Supports development of the following core skills:
Application of number 3.2; Communication 3.1, 3.4 (Task 1)
Application of number 3.2; Communication 3.1, 3.4 (Task 2)
Communication 3.2; Information Technology 3.1, 3.3 (Task 3)

Who consumes 12 tons of salmon, 23 tons of strawberries, 95 000 ice-creams, 190 000 sandwiches, 285 000 cups of tea and coffee, 75 000 pints of beer, 12 500 bottles of champagne and 100 000 lunches in just 13 days? The answer, of course, is the crowds at Wimbledon for the All England Lawn Tennis Championships.

Many catering contracts are year-round but Town and County Catering, a company belonging to the Gardner Merchant group, has met the challenge of providing event catering for visitors to Wimbledon for over 50 years. Though the event lasts only two weeks, the presence of over 370 000 spectators means the catering operation has to be planned well in advance. Event catering is a temporary operation which means that the logistics of transporting equipment and staff, checking power and water supplies, confirming arrangements for cash handling and ensuring that food supplies arrive in the right place are exceptionally complicated.

The catering service has to be provided throughout the day, starting at 6 or 7 a.m. and often running through until midnight. Yet the demand throughout the day is subject to unexpected variables, not least the British weather! A sudden downpour can put catering staff under considerable pressure. A particularly fine day can boost the number of admissions and extend the playing hours until the late evening.

The All England Lawn Tennis and Croquet Club, who host the annual tournament, set stringent criteria for the contract. They monitor the standards of all the catering areas, and periodically obtain tenders from other catering companies to check that Town and County are giving good value for money. Environmental health inspectors from the local authority will also keep a careful check on the health and safety aspects of the operation.

The preparation and provision of food and drink is kept as close to the customers as possible. The main reason for this is that the layout of the courts and surrounding walkways does not allow great freedom of movement, particularly when the presence of crowds is taken into account. Where individual players are performing can make a significant difference to the flow of the crowds and so the siting of individual catering outlets needs to be where there is a demand but also where they will not prove an obstruction.

Customer needs vary from elaborate lunches served in corporate hospitality areas to fast food services offering pizzas and hamburgers. In addition to spectators, food also has to be provided for the players. Given their obvious need to keep in the best possible physical condition, providing for their specific dietary requirements can be demanding. In 1993 Town and County employed a full-time sports dietician for the duration of the tournament.

Meeting the specific requirements of such a major event requires Town and County Catering to commit a huge amount of staff and other resources to a single location. This means that their costs are relatively high and hence they need to charge premium prices for the services they supply.

Your tasks

Marty's Parties Limited is a small company which organises parties and themed events for a range of clients, including both companies and individuals.

In addition to organising the catering for these clients, the company may also be required to provide decorations, props, costumes and entertainment.

The table below shows the five events which they are due to organise on Friday 20 June.

Client	Event	Numbers attending	Time	Venue	Catering requirement	Special requirements
Mr J. Amos	40th birthday party	28	8.30 pm – 12 pm	27 Hart Grove	Buffet (mainly rolls, sandwiches)	Small marquee to be erected in garden
Hope & Leslie (Publishers)	Centenary lunch	100	11.30 am – 2.30 pm	H & L Head Office in Charles Street	Champagne & selection of vol-au-vents	Cake in the shape of a book
Longmarsh Golf Club	Country & Western Evening	120	8 pm – 11.30 pm	Longmarsh Golf Club	Meat and rolls for barbeque	none
Dr R Wells	Retirement event	35	4 pm – 6.30 pm	Upstone College	Buffet (mainly rolls and sandwiches)	Dr Wells has been prominent vegetarian for many years
Mr & Mrs K Loveday	Wedding reception	80	3 pm – 5 pm	St John's Church Hall	Sit-down meal (salads & cold meats	Wedding cake to be collected from baker

1 Discuss the implications for the managers of Marty's Parties Ltd of each of the following events happening in the period leading up to 20 June:

   a) 6 June – Pipers Wines, from whom Marty's Parties buy all alcoholic drinks, offers additional discount on all champagnes for a period of one week only on orders of 6 cases (12 bottles in each) or more

   b) 13 June – Hope & Leslie telephone to ask for two staff to carry trays of food and drink among their guests at the centenary event

   c) 15 June – two of Marty's most experienced staff, an Australian couple, announce that they have to return home immediately due to a family illness, and will probably not return to England

   d) 16 June – a letter arrives from Mrs Loveday saying that the bride and groom-to-be have fallen out. The wedding is therefore off and she wishes to cancel the reception arrangements.

2 Discuss the implications for the managers of Marty's Parties Ltd of each of the following events happening on the day of 20 June:

   a) the weather forecast predicts very heavy rain from about midday

   b) emergency work to repair a gas main leak means that there is no traffic access to Upstone College throughout the day

   c) at 10 a.m. the secretary of Longmarsh Golf Club telephones to say that they have only sold 70 tickets for the country and western evening, and not the 120 expected

   d) Dr Pierre Mangetout, the guest speaker at Dr Wells's retirement event, is delayed at Orly Airport and it is decided to put back the starting time one hour.

3 Choose an event likely to require the services of an outside caterer. Draw up a planning programme for use by the catering company which covers all of the following:

   a) a calendar showing key dates, targets and deadlines

   b) a budget statement for the event

   c) a list of resources required and suppliers to be used

   d) contingency plans in the event of bad weather or other unexpected circumstances

   e) an assignment of roles and responsibilities.

8.5 Planning activity holidays

Develops knowledge and understanding of the following element:
8.2 Plan an event as a team

Supports development of the following core skills:
Communication 3.1, 3.4 (Task 1)
Communication 3.2 (Task 2)

Perhaps as a reaction to too many holidays spent lying on a beach or sitting in a deckchair or perhaps because of warnings about the dangers of too much exposure to the sun, in recent years there has been a marked growth in the popularity of activity holidays.

Planning a new activity holiday requires attention to a wide range of details. Activity holidays carry a higher degree of risk than most others, though there are clearly varying degrees of danger involved. For example, mountaineering is more dangerous than walking, but perhaps safer than hang-gliding.

Many activity centres cater for children and so the quality of the staff they employ is very important. They should have a means of checking that the staff have no previous record of mistreating children in any way. They will also need to demonstrate a high level of skills and an acceptable knowledge of first aid procedures.

Activity centres should be required to record all accidents, including a full explanation of how they happened. Evidence suggests that many accidents to children actually happen during free time. This raises questions about what the correct amount of supervision should be.

Two types of activity holiday which carry particular risks of injury are pony-trekking and water sports. The hot summers of 1990 and 1991 led to an increase of algae in many stretches of fresh water. Anyone swallowing any of this could suffer very serious after effects. Yet there is no legal requirement for staff at activity centres to have first aid qualifications.

The Department for Education has published a document called 'Safety in Outdoor Pursuits' which recommends safety procedures for all centres involved in activity holidays. Most Local Education Authorities also have their own sets of guidelines. The ratio of leaders or instructors to students is an important factor in any safety policy. The training and qualifications of those instructors should also be open to inspection. Many activities are reliant on equipment and this needs to be of a high standard and to be regularly inspected. If you are abseiling down a cliff you want to feel confident that the rope won't break!

Skiing holidays carry a much higher risk of injury than most. The most common injuries suffered are pulled muscles and twisted joints, though broken limbs are not unknown of course. The likelihood of such injuries occurring could be reduced if holiday-makers were to follow a training programme aimed at improving their fitness before they set off. Falls can be caused by incompetence but fatigue is also often a factor. Pre-holiday exercises in the form of running or cycling can improve the stamina of potential skiers and

Activity holiday equipment needs to be of a high standard and regularly inspected.

so lessen the chances of falls resulting from tiredness.

Any plan for an activity holiday scheme should take account of its likely impact on the environment. Some kinds of activity holiday are creating concern because of the impact of new developments on vulnerable environments. Skiing in the Alps is perhaps the best known example. Skiing has grown so rapidly in the area that it is estimated that there are now some 40 000 ski runs and 14 000 ski lifts.

Skiing is totally dependent on snow. In years when there is not enough ski resorts have started to rely on artificial snow machines. Compressed air and water are sprayed at high pressure when temperatures are below feezing. This creates extra snow but is a serious drain on the local water supply. Some methods of making artificial snow also use chemicals to speed the formation of ice crystals. The use of snow machines also means that the skiing season can be extended. This can affect the habitat of local wildlife. It can also increase the damage to the slopes themselves, particularly if people ski over muddy patches. This can accelerate soil erosion and damage wild flowers.

However it is the construction of new ski resorts which perhaps gives the greatest cause for concern. In order to produce suitable ski runs thousands of trees are cleared. Slopes are reshaped, often involving the movement of thousands of tons of earth and the blasting of rocks. This can noticeably increase the dangers from avalanches, since trees give some protection. It has meant that many Alpine roads are covered by a succession of unsightly concrete avalanche shelters. The steel pylons, overhead cables, lifts and tows which are necessary in ski resorts are also visually unattractive.

The construction of new golf courses raises similar concerns. Trees are cut down and earth moved in vast quantities to create hazards. In order to keep the fairways and greens usable, a huge daily supply of water is sprayed over courses in hotter climates. Recent television pictures showed a drought in Zimbabwe, while golf courses in the same country continued to use sprinkler systems. In the United Kingdom, as elsewhere, herbicides and fertilisers are used in large quantities to keep the grass healthy. The result is often a build up of phosphates which eventually drain off into nearby water, increasing algae growth and suffocating fish and other wildlife.

A proposed new activity centre must undergo a feasibility study. Developing a new golf course is seen as an attractive option by leisure developers at the moment, partly because changes in agricultural policy have led farmers to seek alternative uses for land formerly used for cultivation or grazing. In some parts of the country golf clubs have long waiting lists for membership and so there appears to be considerable demand for such facilities. Developers

95

may even get grants to support this change of land use. Some people think this is often a short cut to gaining planning permission for additional building around the course, such as club houses, hotels and apartments. It might be more difficult to gain planning permission to build these in the countryside without the initial construction of a golf course.

Purchasing land or property is often the major cost for companies intending to establish new activity centres. Before deciding to go ahead with such a purchase, however, the company has to establish whether there is sufficient demand for the facilities it intends to provide. The fact that there are waiting lists at most private golf clubs and that you have to book well in advance on many public courses is taken as evidence that there is considerable demand for more golf courses. Yet there would be little point in constructing one which was several hours' drive from the nearest population centre.

In most developments financial backing will be required. The type of development will probably determine how interested investors are. While there may be interest in golf courses with large hotels, intending to attract high-spending business clients, it is more difficult to get funding for municipal courses open to the general public.

The construction of a golf course illustrates the range of costs which have to be met by developers of activity centres. The construction costs involved will depend on the existing terrain. Natural drainage, for example, will save expenditure on ditches and drainage and water systems. Access roads and car parks will need to be put in, as will power supplies and a sewerage system. Some golf centres will also include space-consuming practice facilities, such as driving ranges or putting practice areas. Grants or loans to meet some of these costs are sometimes available from interested sports bodies. However, the majority of the funding is generally raised by persuading other companies to invest in the scheme.

Income once a golf course is operating comes mainly from the fees paid by players, or membership fees as well if the club is private. Many courses cater for more than 50 000 rounds of golf a year and they need to keep players moving reasonably rapidly round the course if they are not to lose money during the course of the year. Driving ranges, which can be completed fairly quickly after planning permission has been granted, are sometimes used to generate income while a new golf course is being constructed elsewhere on the same site.

Your tasks

1 Suppose that you have to organise a party of twenty twelve-year-olds to undertake a cliff top walk.

Below is a list of ten rules which you might draw up for the party to follow. However, some of them would probably be more useful than others. Discuss which six rules you think would be most likely to ensure the safety of your party.

---

1 Always walk in pairs, holding hands.
2 Do not go closer than ten metres to the cliff's edge, unless you are following a path protected on the seaward side by a good fence or wall.
3 Check that you are wearing sensible walking shoes, particularly avoiding high heels or flip-flops.
4 Allow no talking at any time.
5 Make sure that two or more adults are supervising the group at all times.
6 Allow the quicker walkers to go ahead at their own pace.

7   Take a lightweight rucksack for sandwiches, drinks and emergency rations.

8   Do not leave the marked footpath, unless a section of it appears sufficiently damaged to be dangerous.

9   Take along a football for a bit of entertainment along the route.

10   Carry a detailed local map and a compass, and tell a responsible person of your intended route.

---

2 Draw up a similar set of safety rules for a sponsored walk taking in both a canal towpath and a main road.

8.6 Planning a conference – the need for a schedule

Develops knowledge and understanding of the following element:
8.2   Plan an event as a team

Supports development of the following core skills:
Communication 3.2, 3.3; Information Technology 3.3 (Task 1)
Communication 3.2, 3.4; Information Technology 3.1, 3.3 (Task 2)

Conference business has become an important part of the hospitality industry. Larger hotels regard conferences as opportunities to attract a guaranteed number of customers for a period known well in advance. Many attractions, aware of the appeal of their distinctive environments, have developed conference facilities. Some industrial sites with the advantage of city centre locations, like The Whitbread Brewery in London, have converted former business premises for use as conference centres.

The success of a conference has much to do with the liaison which has taken place at the planning stage between the company or organisation involved and those who manage the venue itself. This usually requires the recognition of a single person as the point of contact for the company and another for the venue. Once they have agreed the format of the event, they can then allocate and delegate responsibility for individual areas and formulate a timing plan.

At The Brewery an Account Manager will be appointed to work with each new client. They will initially discuss an agreed timescale, similar to the following example:

1   The client visits the venue to be advised of its full potential

2   A provisional booking made - to be held up to 14 days

3   The booking is confirmed in writing

4   A contract outlining the terms of the booking is sent out

5   The contract is signed and returned with a deposit payment

6   A liaison meeting between Account Manager and client to agree conference details is held 2–3 weeks before the actual event

7   An Event Reservation form is sent to the client

8   Any final changes are discussed

9   The client provides a provisional list of attenders 10 days before the event

10   Final numbers and any seating plan requirements are indicated by the client 3 days before the event.

However, planning a conference is not just about hiring a suitable venue. Much work may have to be done in organising the list of delegates, in supplying them with information about both the conference and the venue, and, most important of all, in making sure that the overall purpose and message of the conference is successfully delivered.

Larger conferences may involve inviting delegates from a number of different companies and regions, as well as a number of guest speakers. The timing of invitations is important, particularly where the people in question are very busy or much in demand as public speakers. Decisions about whether or not to attend may be dependent on other things besides dates. The quality of the information available about the conference may attract or deter potential delegates. The status of the team actually delivering the conference, as well as the guest speakers they have been able to attract, will also influence attendance.

Even where a conference is limited to a particular company and attendance is not voluntary, delegates need to be provided with clear information in advance. This is often produced in a folder which will give details of the conference programme, directions to and around the conference venue and details of restaurants and attractions nearby. Sometimes a list of suggested reading might be included. Many conferences break up the possible monotony of a succession of lectures by including sessions where delegates have to opt for different topics or where they are divided into discussion or work groups. The information pack can help the conference to run more smoothly by giving advanced knowledge of the make-up of working groups or by including return slips asking delegates to nominate the optional sessions they would like to be involved in. If delegates are unlikely to know a number of others attending the conference, name badges can be included with the information folder.

Ensuring that the delegates get the right message from the conference is more difficult. If the presenters and guest speakers are outsiders, it is important to have first-hand experience of how effective they are. It is also vital that they are aware of the intended message of the conference since, otherwise, they may make a very professional but totally irrelevant contribution. Though it is the content of the presenters which is most important, their impact can be reinforced or weakened by the quality of equipment and audio-visual aids available to support them. All equipment has to be tested, on the day it is needed, in the room in which it is to be used. Larger venues will probably have technical specialists on site to advise on equipment, sound and lighting.

Other ways in which the conference message can be put across include using company logos and messages on the conference stationery, using sets designed to emphasise the main theme and including entertainment and social activities designed to make delegates feel the whole event is both well thought out and enjoyable. Small details, like the availability of soft

The conference centre at The Whitbread Brewery, London.

drinks and sweets during conference sessions or the presence of flowers on the tables, can also point to the importance which the organisers attach to the conference.

Your tasks

Identify an area of your school/college which could be used for a conference.

I Prepare a leaflet advertising the venue and explaining the terms of use and the facilities available. You should take into consideration the number and type of staff required, existing regulations and letting arrangements, safety measures and the provision and operation of resources and equipment.

2 Investigate the feasibility of putting on the following conference proposal in your school or college:

A one-day conference for lecturers in travel and tourism

This conference, on the subject of General National Vocational Qualifications, is expected to attract 60 delegates. At this time the qualification is a new one and the conference organisers want the day to be informative, as well as stimulating interest in the new courses.

A reception area will be needed, staffed by someone able to register delegates and provide any information they lack.

Four guest speakers have been invited, two of whom will come by car and two who will need to be met at a station. Microphones will be required and one speaker wishes to illustrate her talk with slides. A 15-minute video also forms part of the morning programme, which will be split up by a coffee break in the middle.

Lunch will be provided for delegates. In the afternoon they will be split into four discussion groups, requiring separate rooms. After a tea break they will return to the main conference room for a question and answer session.

Display tables for free literature are needed, as is space for up to six publishers to exhibit books and resources about travel and tourism during the lunch interval and at the end of the afternoon.

Prepare a short presentation explaining your conclusions and showing how resources in your school or college could be deployed to meet these requirements successfully.

8.7 Hiring premises

Develops knowledge and understanding of the following element:
8.3 Participate in the running of the team event

Supports development of the following core skills:
Communication 3.2, 3.4 (Task 1)
Communication 3.1, 3.2 (Task 2)
Application of number 3.2; Communication 3.1, 3.2; Information Technology 3.1,
  3.2, 3.3 (Task 3)

Any indoor event or function organiser will have to be fully aware of the conditions which apply when they book premises for the occasion. These will usually cover issues like payment, times, types of use, access, insurance, cancellation charges and damage claims.

When a booking is made and confirmed in writing, this usually means the event organisers and the venue owners have entered into a contract. The owners may reserve the right not to accept the booking, particularly if they think it is an inappropriate use of the premises. The owners of a stately home which can be booked for banquets might turn down an application to hold a rugby club dinner. A local authority might turn down an application from a political or pressure group, especially if they thought the occasion might provoke unrest. The application might also be rejected if the numbers involved seemed likely to exceed recommended safety levels.

Once the contract has been entered into, it sometimes proves necessary to cancel the event or function. Hiring agreements, rather like many holiday bookings, may stipulate cancellation charges. These are usually dependent on the length of notice which is given and are often calculated on a percentage of what the full hiring charge would have been. For example a major conference venue might ask for 25 per cent of the agreed fee to be paid if a cancellation takes place six months before the agreed date, but 90 per cent if notification arrives two weeks before hand. If an alternative booking is secured for the same date, the cancellation charge is generally forgotten. Larger venues will normally insist on their right to cancel the booking without any liability in certain extreme circumstances. These would include things like fire or industrial action.

The agreement will usually include information about the level of charges and how and when these are to be paid. The cost to the hirers may consist simply of a flat fee, but if the event is a complex one, there may also be unspecified charges for food and the supply of materials and services. A deposit is usually required to secure a booking with the remaining sums becoming due after the event, when the venue owners send out an invoice for the amount still owed.

Larger venues may have their own regulations about acceptable use. Permission may have to be sought for things like fixing posters to the walls or setting up a stage set. Some activities, such as the showing of films, may require a licence under the Cinema Act; the venue may not be in possession of one. Licences would also be required if it was proposed to have alcohol on sale and if a dance or live music were proposed as part of the programme.

Larger events and functions present some security problems. They attract large numbers of people and yet many will be unfamiliar to each other, making it easy for outsiders to go unnoticed. Event organisers are usually held responsible for property loss or damage to property of people attending the function. Venue owners will often state in their written conditions of hire that they accept no responsibility or liability for loss or damage, unless they have specifically agreed to store equipment in a secure place. The conditions may also state that any damage caused by participants will also render them liable to recompense the owners.

The event organisers would probably be required to provide public liability insurance. This would cover them against any costs incurred if legal proceedings were taken against them as the result of an injury or loss or damage to property suffered by anyone participating in the event. Larger venues, catering for bigger events, may insist on a minimum amount of insurance cover.

The conditions of use may also cover a number of safety and security issues. Where a complex electrical operation is needed, for example for a theatrical performance, there may be rules about safety fittings, power connections and cable routes. There will probably be fire regulations to comply with, insisting that fire exit signs are kept clearly visible, extinguishers remain accessible and exits and gangways are kept free from obstruction. Smoking may be banned in some areas. For events which require hired contractors to set them up beforehand, the venue owners may insist on security passes being issued to all bona fide workers.

Your tasks

A travelling theatre company wishes to stage a public performance in your school or college.

1   Draw up a list of terms and conditions of hire which the company must agree to before they are permitted to hire your premises.
    You may need to consult regulations already established by your school or college governing body.

2   Contact either an individual performer or a dance, drama or music group.
    Send them a copy of your terms and conditions, and a letter asking them to comment on the feasibility of using the premises on these terms and conditions. Discuss their responses.

3   Using these responses as your starting point, draw up arrangements for an actual performance, allocating different groups responsibilities for:
    ● negotiating content
    ● agreeing cost and admission charges
    ● planning and producing publicity
    ● liaising with outside agencies over health, safety and security
    ● arranging seating plans, issue of tickets, collection of admission money.

8.8 Planning schedules

Develops knowledge and understanding of the following element:
8.3 Participate in the running of the team event

Supports development of the following core skills:
Communication 3.1 (Task 1)
Communication 3.2, 3.3, 3.4 (Task 2)
Communication 3.1, 3.2; Information Technology 3.3 (Task 3)
Communication 3.1; Information Technology 3.4 (Task 4)

Planning events of any size requires extensive consultation. This will generally begin on an informal basis but once there is agreement that the event should take place more formal meetings have to be held. In addition to the organisation of the event itself there may need to be consultation with outside agencies such as the police, the local authority and the fire service. Larger events, such as festivals, are often managed by committees. Sometimes smaller sub-groups are appointed to plan specific tasks.

Below is an extract from a report written in 1978, describing a suggested sequence of planning stages for a committee organising a festival, commemoration or anniversary:

Festival Planning Report

1 Form small initial group for early discussion and making provisional outline of project.
2 Consult local Regional Tourist Board and Local Authorities.
3 Form official Management Committee and ensure membership includes necessary skills in law, finance and insurance and representatives of appropriate sections of community. Consider possibility Superior Council to determine policy and/or patrons of substantial local or national stature. Consider how work can be divided and decision-making efficiency improved by formation of sub-committees.
4 Consider possible sources of funds from private donations, grants or guarantees from commercial and industrial communities, Local Authorities, official tourist bodies, Arts Council of Great Britain (see point 7 below), etc. In the light of plans made (see point 5 below) estimate total expenditure and sum to be recouped, i.e. net cost.
5 Make plans for nature, scale and length of celebrations which may have to be modified in the light of financial and other support which can be reasonably expected. Relate plans to availability of halls, theatres, weather expectation, hotel accommodation, catering and transport facilities, etc.
6 Consider whether project justifies or needs engagement of professionals for artistic direction, management, performances, publicity, public relations, etc.
7 Consider whether the cultural and artistic element of the celebration justifies applying for financial support from the Arts Council of Great Britain, or, alternatively, from the Scottish, Welsh or Northern Ireland Arts Councils or one of the regional Arts Associations.
8 Consider whether the benefit to the public justifies application for registration as a charity with consequent tax advantages particularly when continuing existence envisaged.
9 Consider whether scale and nature of operations contemplated suggest formation of company incorporated with financial liability.

10 Make certain there is adequate insurance against accident and other risks.

11 Begin promotional publicity early: Leaflets, posters, brochures, etc., and ensure their useful and appropriate distribution. Seek publicity from media. Consult official tourist bodies. Is any area at home or abroad likely to have special interest? Bear in mind that foreign tourists alone will not guarantee success; visits from within a country will form the basis of success and financial support. Consider advisability of allocation of block bookings to travel agents, coach operators, etc., and encouragement of package tours. Leaflet to contain information re hotels, restaurants, transport facilities, etc. Adopt symbol or emblem.

12 Consider advisability of attracting associated events.

13 Explore all means of recouping expenses including sale of brochures and programmes and advertising space, admission charges, bar and catering and souvenirs.

14 Consultation with police and motoring organisations.

This is a very comprehensive list and includes some requirements which might not be essential in the planning of small events.

Your tasks

I Select a theme which would make an appropriate focus for a one-day festival to be held in your school or college.
You might choose to focus the festival on one of the following:
- a famous event from the past
- a local celebrity
- a particular art form like film or sculpture.

2 Use the planning sequence taken from the report on festivals to help you to decide on the size and membership of a planning committee for your festival.
Draw a diagram which indicates the responsibilities of the members of the planning committee and which also shows the lines of communication which will need to be established.

3 Set a suitable date for the festival. Use a calendar to draw up a planning schedule which gives a detailed indication of when consultation and action will be needed, and which shows who will be responsible for initiating it.

4 Review your schedule to ensure that your festival or commemorative event is manageable in terms of the resources you have available. Modify what you intend to include in the light of this review, and then allocate group responsibilities for the planning and running of the event.

8.9 Assessing hazards and risks for an event

Develops knowledge and understanding of the following element:
8.4 Evaluate individual, team and event performance

Supports development of the following core skills:
Communication 3.2 (Task 1)
Communication 3.1 (Task 2)
Information Technology 3.3, 3.4 (Task 3)

In evaluating whether or not an event was a success, the organisers will want to see if anything went wrong which might have been avoided. They may identify a number of potential hazards the event created. They will then have to decide whether they took sufficient measures to reduce the risk from these hazards to the people taking part. The terms 'risk' and 'hazard' need clear explanation:

- a hazard is anything with the potential to inflict harm, such as a fire;
- a risk is the likelihood that the hazard will actually cause harm.

In other words, a hazard, like a fire, will be less of a risk if fire extinguishers and staff fully trained in their use are available at the event.

There are a number of risks associated with the running of any event. If it is to be successful, these must be carefully analysed, and financial and physical steps taken to reduce the risks as much as possible. Decisions will have to be taken by those responsible for the event about what is an acceptable level of risk and also about liability in the event of anything going wrong.

The first task of event organisers is to identify potential hazards. Clearly not all hazards have the same potential to cause harm. A patch of muddy ground near the entrance to an open air pop festival will probably be regarded as less serious than the number of people intended to use a hastily erected temporary grandstand. The following table, produced by the National Outdoor Events Association, suggests a hazard rating on a scale of 1 to 10 for a number of possible event occurrences.

Category	Occurrence
1	Generation of low toxicity dust or fumes in open area
2	Casual labour working under tight supervision
4	Failure of light duty temporary barrier
4	Casual labour working under loose supervision
5	Minor floor fault
6	Minor vandalism
6	Skilled operative working at height
7	Breakdown of food hygiene control procedures
7	Collapse of low, lightweight structure
7	Fire in open area
8	Collapse of low rostrum or staging
8	Arson during closed period
9	Failure of heavy duty temporary barrier
10	Fire in enclosed area
10	Collapse of grandstand, tower or other high structure
10	Congestion of panicking or emotive public

In the same way that the hazards of running an event can be assessed in terms of how dangerous generally they are, so different types of event can also be rated in terms of their potential risk to participants. Using a 1 to 10 scale similar to that shown in assessing hazard potential, the following table shows the potential level of risk generally associated with certain types of event.

Category	Event
1	Small garden party (50–100 guests)
2	Sedentary sport or quiet event, e.g. bowls tournament
3	Lively events or sport with fixed seating, e.g. tennis
5	Emotive sports in permanent stands, e.g. football
6	Exciting event – part seats, part standing, e.g. racing
7	Temporary stands/enclosures – aggressive event, e.g. boxing
8	Highly emotive event – audience participation, e.g. political or religious rally
9	Pop concerts
10	Raves

However, none of these ways of assessing risk is satisfactory when considered alone. The most important factor in assessing risks at an event is the number of people who are likely to attend. A pop concert attended by 25 people would probably present less risk than a tennis tournament attended by a crowd of 25 000.

If the event is likely to attract sufficiently large numbers for this to present a risk in itself, certain measures can be taken to control the numbers. These could include the methods by which people are admitted. For example:

- admission might be by ticket only;
- admission might be limited to advanced bookings only;
- seating might be individually numbered and specifically allocated.

Other controls might include:
- the use of barriers and fencing to segregate sections of the crowd;
- the use of stewards; the use of video surveillance and two-way radio;
- extra supervision and direction at doors, entrances and gangways.

Another factor which increases or reduces risk, regardless of the nature of the event, is whether or not alcohol is on sale on the site where the event is taking place. As with the numbers attending, alcohol is a factor that increases the risks for events which in any case have the power to generate high emotions.

There are four main stages involved in risk management. These are:

1 identifying the nature of the hazards involved
2 assessing the degree of risk these hazards present, either personally or by seeking expert advice
3 choosing the best methods of eliminating hazards where possible and otherwise reducing the risks they present to a minimum
4 evaluating how successful the measures taken were in ensuring that the event passed off without harm caused to people, property or the environment.

Your tasks

1 List all the hazards presented by an event you are running and place them in categories according to how serious you think each one is.

2 Discuss what actions you need to take in order to minimise the risks to any participants in the event.

3 Suppose that as a condition for allowing your event to run, an independent inspection team must assess the site and facilities both before and during the event. Use appropriate computer software in order to design two inspection forms or check lists which the inspectors might use to monitor both the planning and running of the event.

8.10 Evaluating the performance of festival security staff

Develops knowledge and understanding of the following element:
8.4　Evaluate individual, team and event performance

Supports development of the following core skills:
Communication 3.2, 3.4 (Task 1)
Communication 3.1, 3.4 (Task 2)
Communication 3.2 (Task 3)
Communication 3.2 (Task 4)

Open air festivals and concerts often attract large crowds, and therefore require responsible and well-trained security staff to ensure that everything goes smoothly. There has been a large increase in the number of security firms advertising their services. Much public concern has been expressed about the quality of service offered by some of these companies and there have been calls for stricter controls to be applied to them.

Security firms seeking to establish and maintain a good reputation will often be active members of a relevant security association. Such companies sometimes specialise in different aspects of security such as stewarding, ticket inspection, segmentation, seat allocation and evacuation procedures.

Below is a checklist which festival organisers might use in evaluating the suitability of security staff.

1　Do they have full knowledge of medical and emergency organisations on the site?
2　Are they sufficiently familiar with evacuation procedures?
3　Are they sensitive to people in distress or difficulty?
4　Are they confident enough to deal with problems?
5　Will they stay calm in a crisis?
6　Do they have any record of violence or dishonesty?
7　Are there an adequate number with first aid qualifications?

Where large crowds are involved it is important that security staff can be easily identified.

This generally means they will wear some kind of uniform and will display an identity badge which includes an up-to-date photograph. This enables people needing help to pick them out more quickly, as well as reassuring people that they have genuine security responsibilities. This is particularly important where sensitive issues, such as searching people's bags, is a requirement for admission.

If there is a need to search people's property, security staff must be able to handle this situation with sensitivity. It must be carried out at the entrance to the site, and the reason for the search should be clearly stated. For example, there may be a ruling that no one is allowed to bring alcoholic drinks into an event and therefore bags may need to be searched to check that this is not happening. However, some types of search, such as those looking for illegal drugs, may only be carried out by the police.

Security staff can prevent people from bringing prohibited items into an event. However the organisers have to give notice of the ban beforehand. Any property confiscated has to be held in safe custody and must be returned in the same condition. Security staff are not allowed to take money from participants unless they have been authorised to collect admission fees. Wherever any money is accepted, they must always provide a ticket or receipt to indicate exactly what sum was handed over.

The real test of whether security staff have performed their role effectively often comes when they are confronted by violence or disorder. How they react in these circumstances can make or mar an event. Unfortunately in some circumstances they may be required to use a certain amount of force to prevent trouble. The law allows them to use 'reasonable force' where it is essential. If the security staff do their job well, any such incidents will be reported immediately to the security controller. Serious incidents, particularly if they involve injury or if they result in an individual being detained should be reported to the police immediately.

Your tasks

Easthampton Music Festival is held once a year on Easthampton Common. This year it is decided to hire a new security firm for the event, as the company responsible for last year's event, No Bother Ltd, failed to live up to their name. Below are the thoughts of a number of interested parties, about what sort of service they are looking for this year.

Marcus Pott, chairperson of the Festival organising committee:
'We must make sure that no cash is unaccounted for this year. We didn't receive everything which should have been due from ticket sales and concessions last year. We also lost money as a result of people getting in by climbing over fences and not paying admission. That said, we must not incur such a large fee for security that we're left with no profit. We want good behaviour, sensible parking and control of the site so that it's not left in the complete mess we faced a year ago.'

Juanita Pye, holder of the catering concessions for the Festival:
'I'd like to see much more security in evidence than there was last year. Some of the trading sites we'd agreed last year were not accessible when we arrived. We also found other traders who had not paid concessions to operate on the site were allowed to set up stalls. We had some trouble with people refusing to pay for food. Two of our van drivers reported

difficulty in getting on to the site to deliver fresh supplies. One food outlet was broken into during the night. Food was stolen and equipment damaged.'

Maisie Glover, regular attender at the Festival:
'I could do without the long queues we had to endure last year before we were admitted. Views of the stage were fairly limited unless you arrived for each day's performance pretty early. Generally there wasn't much trouble, apart from one or two incidents where security staff were a bit heavy-handed. They were much too fussy about camping and fire-lighting regulations. After all, people were out to enjoy themselves and didn't need to be hassled about petty rules.'

Phyllis Ling, local organiser for the St John Ambulance Brigade:
'One or two cases we saw last year were very slow in reaching us. A girl with a very bad cut had been told by a security guard that there was no first aid on the site and that she'd have to find her own way to hospital. We would have been happier to be sited further away from some of the food outlets, since these attracted crowds, making us less accessible and less visible.'

1 Write a brief report summarising the main weaknesses in security identified at last year's Easthampton Music Festival.

2 Suggest some factors which might have contributed to the failure to provide security of the highest standard.

3 List the main criteria which you think should apply in determining which company should be offered a contract to manage the security of the current year's festival.

4 Draw up an agreement, stating the conditions which any company wishing to be awarded the contract, will have to meet.

Glossary

base rate   the rate which banks use to determine the interest they will charge to borrowers

bequests   sums of money or property left in a will to another person or organisation

bond   a sum of money held on behalf of a company, to be used to refund their customers should the company go out of business

branding   using a name or trade mark to make individual products easy to distinguish from their competitors, and to establish them in the minds of existing and potential customers

capital works   major fixed investment usually associated with buildings or equipment and often funded by long term loans or directly out of company profits

cash flow   the movement of money received and paid out by a business

charitable trust   a non-profit-making organisation overseeing the use of funds often donated specifically for the upkeep and management of property or estates

compulsory competitive tendering (CCT)   a requirement of the Local Government Act (1988) setting up a process by which some local authority services, such as leisure provision, have to be defined in a contract for which private companies wishing to manage these services can compete

contingency plan   a plan made in order to be ready for the occurrence of some chance or unexpected situation

crime audit   a detailed assessment of the crime risks in a specific location and the remedial actions which these might require

deeds of covenant   legal agreements usually covering a set period and often involving the contribution of funds to another person or organisation

directives   decisions passed on as instructions from one organisation having authority over others

documentation   all the written paperwork which supports a business transaction

endowment   money which is settled on a specific property in order to maintain and restore it

English Tourist Board   a national government-funded organisation aiming to encourage the British to take more holidays in England and to improve the facilities available to them when they do

ethos   the type of behaviour and atmosphere which is characteristic of an organisation

freehold   property which the owner is free to dispose of or pass on as an inheritance

heritage   sites, buildings and artefacts reflecting the achievements and way of life of our ancestors

job description   a statement of the duties and responsibilities which the holder of a specific job is expected to carry out

legacy   money or personal property left in a will

liability	responsibility to protect clients against risk
logo	a symbol, picture or design used to identify a company or product
market value	the current price which potential purchasers are willing to pay for goods or services
media	means by which information is passed on to the public, for example newspapers, radio, television
networked	linked into a system of computer terminals which can pass information to one another
occupancy rate	a means of measuring how successfully hotels are performing by calculating the percentage of rooms occupied and whether each of these is a single or double occupancy
person specification	a description of the skills and qualities expected of suitable recruits for an advertised job
premium payment	a single sum of money paid for insurance
private sector	businesses owned and operated by private individuals and firms
privatise	to convert a business or organisation from government funding to private ownership
pro forma	a document or form in which the layout and wording has been standardised
public sector	organisations and businesses financed by government funds
regeneration	the rebuilding and revitalising of areas such as city centres
remortgage	borrowing an additional sum of money using the increased value of property as security
retail travel	the process of selling travel arrangements directly to customers
security	land or property offered as a guarantee against the repayment of a loan
source markets	the area from which potential customers are derived
subsidiary	a less important branch of a company, but one which contributes to their overall profit
tagging	a system of using labels attached to goods which set off an alarm if they are removed from the premises
target markets	the consumer groups to which a company is aiming to sell its products and services
Tourist Information Centre	a centre providing information about transport, accommodation and attractions in the surrounding area
turnover	the money value of a company's total sales and other income over a specified period
viability	the likelihood of a business or scheme being successful
voluntary sector	organisations funded by members, voluntary contributions and charities